Hilarie Oliver
7310 35th Street Ct W Apt 2
University Place, WA 98466-4433

D0021663

the Fellowship of Ghosts

The author in the mountains above Krossbu

the Fellowship *of* Ghosts

A Journey Through the Mountains of Norway

PAUL WATKINS

NATIONAL GEOGRAPHIC

WASHINGTON, D.C.

Also By Paul Watkins

Thunder God
The Forger
The Story of My Disappearance
Archangel
Stand Before Your God
The Promise of Light
In the Blue Light of African Dreams
Calm at Sunset, Calm at Dawn
Night Over Day Over Night

the Fellowship of Ghosts

Copyright © 2004 Paul Watkins
Map copyright © 2004 National Geographic Society

Library of Congress Cataloging-in-Publication Data available upon request
ISBN: 0-7922-6799-0

One of the world's largest nonprofit scientific and educational organizations, the National Geographic Society was founded in 1888 "for the increase and diffusion of geographic knowledge." Fulfilling this mission, the Society educates and inspires millions every day through its magazines, books, television programs, videos, maps and atlases, research grants, the National Geographic Bee, teacher workshops, and innovative classroom materials. The Society is supported through membership dues, charitable gifts, and income from the sale of its educational products. This support is vital to National Geographic's mission to increase global understanding and promote conservation of our planet through exploration, research, and education.

For more information, please call 1-800-NGS LINE (647-5463)
or write to the following address:

National Geographic Society
1145 17th Street N.W.
Washington, D.C. 20036-4688 U.S.A.

Visit the Society's Web site at www.nationalgeographic.com.

Printed in U.S.A.
Design by Melissa Farris

This book is for ECW and OLW.

CONTENTS

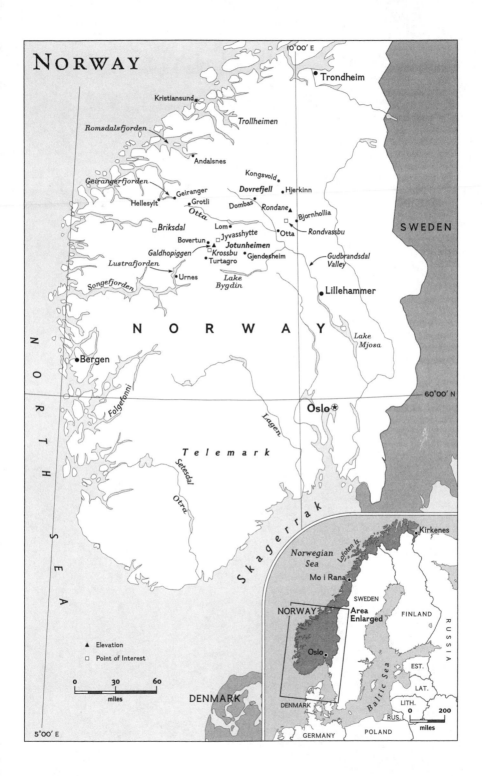

NORWAY

Trondheim

Kristiansund

Romsdalsfjorden

Trollheimen

Andalsnes

Kongsvold
Dovrefjell Hjerkinn

Geirangerfjorden
Geiranger Grotli
Hellesylt Dombas Rondane
Otta Rondvassbu
□ *Briksdal* Lom Jyvasshytte
Bovertun □ Otta
Galdhopiggen □ *Jotunheimen*
□ Krossbu Gjendesheim
Lustrafjorden Turtagro
Songefjorden Urnes Lake
Bygdin

Bjornhollia

SWEDEN

*Gudbrandsdal
Valley*

Lillehammer

N O R W A Y

Lake
Mjosa

Bergen

Folgefonni

60°00′ N

Oslo ✧

Lagen

T e l e m a r k

Setesdal

Otra

S k a g e r r a k

▲ Elevation
□ Point of Interest

0   30   60
miles

DENMARK

10°00′ E

5°00′ E

Kirkenes

*Norwegian
Sea*

Lofoten Is.

Mo i Rana

SWEDEN

NORWAY **Area
Enlarged**

FINLAND

R
U
S
S
I
A

Oslo

DENMARK

EST.

Baltic Sea

LAT.

LITH.
0   200
RUS.   miles

GERMANY   POLAND

N
O
R
T
H

S
E
A

Chapter One

Deep-Sea Dreamer

MY FIRST JOURNEY TO NORWAY BEGAN WITH AN ACCIDENT that almost killed me on the deck of a deep-sea fishing boat.

It was the summer of my first year at university. I had traded my Harris Tweed jacket, the musty smell of Sterling Library, and the sound of the Whiffenpoofs crooning at Mory's in New Haven for jeans pockholed with welding sparks, the reek of gutted fish and the constant rolling hammering of diesel engines.

The boat was a scallop dragger; a ninety-foot Western rig out of Wanchese, North Carolina, which came up to Newport, Rhode Island, every summer. The captain was a balding, round-faced man named Billy, whose temper was so fierce that he had a reputation for losing half his crew every time he came back to port.

It was my third trip. We were two days out on a ten-day voyage, working five hours on, four hours off, without a break to this routine. After a while, you lose track of how long you have been gone. You learn that time runs differently when you are out of sight of land. The quicker you settle into a routine, the less punishing it becomes. You wander through daydreams so intense that you wake up surprised to find yourself out on the water.

Besides cutting out the scallops, which we hauled up in two huge steel dredges, my job at the end of every watch was to go below deck to the freezer room. There, I would chop out slots in the ice for the linen bags in which we stored the rubbery scallop meats.

It was hot up on deck. If you left your rubber boots out in the sun, they would stick to the iron deck plates. Whenever someone had to go down into the engine room, another person had to stand up at the top of the ladder. This was to make sure the one who went down to deal with the monstrous Caterpillar engines did not pass out from the heat.

I was always glad to get down into the ice room. The first thing I did was scoop up a handful of the near-freezing water that sluiced back and forth across the concrete ice room floor and wash the sweat off my face. This was about the only chance I had to be alone, and the cold would jolt me from the waking dream that filled my days when I was out to sea.

The ice room was my own tiny kingdom. I had chopped a seat into the wall of the ice, and when the work was done I would sit there for a while, like an emperor on a throne, surveying my frozen domain.

If it was stormy, waves would sometimes spill into the ice room. Then the place would fill with condensation and I would find myself enveloped in a fog so thick I could not see from one end of the room to the other. I had been warned by my watch mate, a veteran fisherman named Arneson, always to wait until both of the dredges were on deck before climbing back up the ladder. The dredges were sixteen feet across at the base and weighed as much as a small car. In rough weather, they would swing across the deck and crash together like giant cymbals.

On this day, I had just finished bedding down the scallops in their cocoons of ice. The boat pitched and rolled in the swells of an oncoming storm. I stood at the base of the ladder, hearing the whine of the winches as they hauled up the dredges. They had been down deep. There were rumors on our watch that we were out by the continental shelf, but we never really knew where we were. The captain liked to keep it secret where we fished, so he could keep his prized scallop beds to himself.

I heard the dredges clank against the side, then a rattle as the hooks were set to lift them onto the deck. I waited for the crashes as the both dredges came to rest on the deck plates, then climbed quickly up the twelve rungs of the ladder. I stuck my head up out of the hatch.

All I can remember thinking is, "Where is the sky?"

The next thing I knew, I was back down in the ice room. I was on my hands and knees, spitting out sand. I had no idea what I was doing there and could not understand why I wasn't up on deck. I felt as if someone were playing a practical joke on me. As I was trying to get back on my feet, I noticed that the inch-deep water which covered the ice room floor had turned pink. Looking down at my chest, I saw that I was covered in blood.

Only then did I grasp that something was wrong with me, but I had no sensation of pain. My body hummed the way a sewing machine does before the needle jabs. I started shaking. Slowly, I lifted up my T-shirt. There was a bruise on my right side, the skin blotchy from blood vessels burst beneath the skin. But the skin itself was unbroken. I began to explore my arms, then my legs, hunting for the source of the blood.

When, I touched a hand against my face, my right index finger went straight through the lower part of my cheek and touched the hard, slippery surface of my jawbone. Then I realized it was not sand I had been spitting out. It was my teeth.

When Arneson came to find out what had happened, he found me crawling around and trying to gather up the fragments of broken bone. He came down the ladder and tried to get a look at the wound in my face, but I pushed him away and told him to help me find my teeth. I must have fainted then, because the next thing I remember is Arneson trying to carry me up the ladder. Then I fainted again and woke up in my bunk with Captain Billy breathing in my face.

He asked me how I felt and I said I was fine. When he asked me if I could still work, I told him I could. I said all this because I wanted everything to be back to normal. If I went back to work, it would be a sign that things weren't serious. Also, I was new on this crew, and knew that injuries were common among fishermen. I had been shown the scars of everything from bullet holes to shark bites to the marble-smooth bumps of places where fingers had been. I didn't want to quit.

I asked Arneson what the hell had happened to me. He explained that one of the dredges had been safely on the deck, but the other one had bounced and was still swinging through the air when I stuck my head above the hatch. The corner of the dredge hit me in the face, shoving back my jaw and shearing off my rear teeth. Later, a dentist told me that my jaw had probably been dislocated, but that striking the floor of the ice room must have relocated it.

It took two days for the sewing machine hum to leave my body. By that time I had learned that only my back teeth were broken. I could not close my mouth, or a feeling exactly like biting a piece of tinfoil when you have fillings would jab into my brain. I could find no way of bandaging the hole in my cheek, so I just dabbed it with iodine every time I went out on watch, staining my face jaundice yellow.

The biggest problem was that I could not chew my food. The cook, an old black man named Carlton, fixed me grits for every meal. I found that if I mashed cooked vegetables with a fork and stirred it into the grits, I could get it down.

We stayed out for another week, and I had all the time in the world to think about the damage that had been done. Running my tongue along the once-smooth line of my back teeth was like licking the rim of a broken pottery mug.

At first I tried to convince myself that it wouldn't cost much to put me right. The more times I played it over in my head, the less of a problem it all seemed to be. If I had gone on dreaming like this, I would probably have broken down completely when it came to learning what was actually required.

It was Arneson who kept me sane. He told me it looked bad. It would take surgery to fix me up and the fact that I was not in a lot of pain meant that some of the broken teeth were dead. They would have to be root-canaled. He quoted Nietzsche, saying that what had failed to kill me would only make me stronger. Initially, I took this for nothing but cruelty, but slowly I began to understand that he was helping me. Once he felt sure that I had faced the facts, he worked to keep my mind off my troubles. We would lie in our bunks, which were like coffins with one side pulled away, and he would tell me about his childhood home in Norway, in a place called Andalsnes.

Arneson had emigrated with his parents in the late 1950s, but had never been back. When I asked him why, he had trouble finding an answer. He knew the reason well enough, but was nervous about putting it into words. For him, the whole of Norway had settled in his mind into a place of such fantastic beauty that he was afraid to return, in case the reality turned out to be a sad departure from the dream he had made for himself. It was as if the real Norway of his childhood had sunk beneath the strange green water of the fjords and a new, magical world had risen in its place. Out here on this floating slaughterhouse where he made his living, the magical place was worth more to him than what might be the truth.

I understood exactly how he felt, and told him about my own family, who are all from the southwest corner of Wales. They live scattered among the windswept beaches and purple-heathered hills of places with names like Abergwaun and Dynbich-Y-Pescod. My parents emigrated from there around the same time as Arneson's, and although I was not born in Wales I visited there often. In between visits, I felt the almost tidal pull of a bloodline woven into the fabric of all things Welsh. The longer I spent away from Wales, the more beautiful the place became in my mind. How dreary it was on those occasions when I visited, as the westbound train trundled in the rain through Cardiff station, to feel the dream made ludicrous. Eventually, the dream would return. It always did. But each time it was more of a dream.

I could not blame Arneson for keeping such a fantasy alive. His descriptions of the mountains rising thousands of feet sheer out of the fjords removed me so completely from the clamor of the engines and the dangerous monotony of dredges and knives and my staggering path across the storm-pitched deck that I promised myself I would go there. To Andalsnes. To see for myself.

In the meantime, with thoughts like this out in the open, we had no choice but to laugh at our confessions. We called ourselves the Deep-Sea Dreamers, and looked with quiet pity on the men whose minds and bodies remained anchored to this unforgiving iron boat.

TWO MONTHS LATER, with a few weeks still to go before the start of the new school year, Captain Billy told us he was heading back to the Carolinas. The hurricane season was coming. Soon it would be flailing at New England with its dreaded nor'easters, and a few boats always went down this time of year.

That meant the end of work for his Newport-based crew. For me, it came just in time. Since the accident I had not been sleeping well.

Almost every night, just as I was drifting off, I would be jolted awake by the sensation of something lunging at me, as if I were being attacked. I had no idea what it was or what to make of it. I told myself I was just tired of being out on the water.

The same day Captain Billy headed south, I boarded a plane bound for Oslo. From there I'd make my way to Andalsnes.

By then, most of Arneson's predictions has come true. Surgery. Root canals. Porcelain and gold crowns. Thousands of dollars in medical bills. During all those hours in the dentist's chair, through the sound of drills and the bitter taste of novocaine trickling down the back of my throat, the promise to visit Andalsnes had glimmered in front of me with the holographic vividness of a Holy Grail. I hoped Arneson was as right about the beauty of the place as he had been about the damage to my teeth.

I'd had no time to read up on Norway, and what I already knew wasn't much. In between fishing trips, my time on land had usually been spent asleep, with the ocean still rocking like a ball bearing in the white dish of my skull. I didn't mind that I knew so little about where I was headed. In fact, it seemed better not to know. It was like walking toward a mirage, which was exactly how my time on the boats had begun to seem—a flicker of images fragmented by the smashed-glass glitter of light on water. I was leaving one dream and heading toward another.

THE GLASS AND STEEL and blonde wood structure of Norway's Gardemoen Airport seemed to radiate a sense of calm. Airport personnel rode up and down the concourse on two-wheeled scooters. They moved with the dignity of swans across a lake, aloof and detached from us travelers, who blinked the jet lag from our bleary eyes.

I stepped off the airport express train at the Oslo Sentralstasjon just in time to board another bound for Andalsnes. I barely had time to notice the city as our dusty red wagons clanked out into the countryside. It was a bright morning as I traveled up the gently rolling Gudbrandsdal valley, skirting the jade green water of Lake Mjosa. The fields had already been cut, and the honey-colored stubble took on an almost liquid quality in the late summer light. For the first time in as long as I could remember, my mind was at peace.

The closer we came to Andalsnes, the more the gentle ground gave way to steeper slopes as mountains closed in on the valley. The wide, still water of Lake Mjosa was replaced by the whitecaps of the River Lagen. In place of the modern buildings I had glimpsed as we passed through Lillehammer and Hamar, I now saw farmsteads with turfed roofs and tarred-log walls. Waterfalls plunged out of the rocks, haloing us in rainbows.

I thought, No wonder Arneson didn't come back. It would be all too easy to persuade yourself that you had imagined a landscape like this. I found myself trying to memorize the names of places we passed through—Otta, Vinstra, Dombas—as if to fend off a lingering uneasiness that I might blink and find myself back on the boat, with nothing more than a strange dream to tell Arneson when we next went out on watch.

It took almost six hours to reach Andalsnes, by which time the vertically rising mountains of the Romsdal valley had split the landscape between daylight and the dusk of shadows.

Everything I had brought with me was jammed into an old canvas rucksack, including a flimsy one-man tent, too many books, and a mess kit dating back to the First World War.

Descending from the train, I shouldered my pack, whose once-brown leather straps were stained almost black by the sweat of previous travels. I asked a sleepy stationmaster how far it was to the campsite.

He was sitting on a bench, arms folded across his dark blue–uniformed chest, thoughtfully twitching his mustache as if trying to dislodge it from his upper lip.

"Perhaps half an hour?" I asked, hoping to jog his mind into action.

His chin jerked upward. "No," he said decisively, but that was all. He aimed his arm toward the river, looking like the ghost of Christmas Yet To Come showing Scrooge his own gravestone.

Andalsnes was smaller than I'd thought it would be, and more modern in its appearance. I wondered how much it had changed since Arneson's time. Hiking toward the edge of town, I passed rows of unimpressive, functional-looking houses. This architecture seemed almost an act of surrender—as if the mountains were so overshadowing that nothing could be done to compete with their presence.

I crossed the Rauma River to the Andalsnes campsite, which fanned out across a field at the edge of the water. After pitching my tent and crawling into my sleeping bag, I was suddenly exhausted. All the energy I had saved up to reach this place had been spent, leaving me with nothing to continue. The truth was, I had given no thought to continuing. I had only wanted to get here. Now that I had arrived, with only a day or two before I had to turn around and begin the journey home, I felt a great emptiness inside.

Even though I was too tired to read or to eat, my thoughts still rattled forward without direction. Through the mosquito netting, my head propped up on my books, I watched evening fill the valley with a brassy light, which turned to copper, then to poppy red, and finally only the mountains in the distance held on to the glow of the sun. Far above in that other world, tiger stripes of snow filled the gullies. I wondered how it might be to climb them, and if it could even be done.

Finally, just as I was about to fall asleep, that thing lunged at me again. It startled me wide awake, and I lay there for a long time, trying unsuccessfully to figure out what it was. I had clung to the belief that quitting the boats and traveling here might rid me of the problem, like a cripple on a pilgrimage to Lourdes. Now I saw how mistaken I had been.

The sounds of the campground—the softly played radios and purr of languages I did not understand—all faded away in the dove-gray twilight. Soon the valleys grew quiet. No cars or trains. No sound of birds or barking dogs. Only the rustle of water, and mountains breathing from the granite vaults of their lungs.

THE NEXT DAY I CLIMBED the Aksla mountain, which rose from the eastern edge of town. It formed one edge of a range of hills, whose blunt-topped peaks snubbed the sky like a row of huge, bared teeth. A few houses clung precariously to its lower slopes, which almost gave the mountain a sense of movement, as if it were rising from the ground, shrugging off the luminous green grass of the valley below.

The path zigzagged crazily up through groves of spindly pines, gradually thinning out until there were no trees at all, only moss-patched stones and beds of pale green lichen spreading out across the high ground. Snow clung to the shadowy places, chilling the breeze that blew across its dirty back.

After months of stilted walking on the deck of Captain Billy's boat, the pain of climbing, particularly in my thigh muscles, was so intense that the only way I could convince myself to continue was to take a kind of perverse pleasure in the agony.

I had used up the water in my canteen before I was even out of the poplars. As soon as I reached the first patch of snow, I filled my canteen from a tiny stream that plipped from the ice. I drank and drank until my thirst was finally quenched, then sat back with a bloated stomach on a bed of lichen, feeling it crackle beneath me.

The town below had been reduced to a cluster of Playmobil structures, and the train trundling back toward Oslo looked like a string of red licorice in the distance. Beyond stood the Trollveggen mountains. Unlike the sheared-off hill that I was climbing, the Trollveggen spiked the horizon with the jaggedness of waves in a Hokusai painting. I wished Arneson could have been there, so that he would have known that even his dreams did not match what I could see before me now.

I could not linger, either on the mountain or in Norway. With only two weeks to go before the start of the new school year, I began my journey home.

It took me all day to reach the town of Otta, which lies about halfway between Andalsnes and Oslo. I planned to travel on from there the following morning, and spend a few days roaming around Oslo.

The path to the campsite led through a sour-smelling lumber-yard, where sprinklers chip-chip-chipped back and forth, keeping the logs damp. The campsite itself had been reduced to mud by a summer of rain and car tires. I rented a small wooden cabin and installed myself in one of the two bunks. I thought about heading back into town, just to sit at the station café or maybe find a movie theater, but it had begun to rain and the town had not looked promising, so I stayed put.

Lulled almost to sleep by the patter of rain on the roof, I was suddenly jolted awake as the waking nightmare lunged at me again. Suddenly the cozy bunk became claustrophobically small, reminding me too much of the bunk room on the boat. I slept with the door open, rain blowing in, darkening the chafed bare wood of the floor.

The next morning, while I waited for the train to Oslo, I picked up a brochure for hiking in the Rondane mountains, for which Otta was apparently the central jumping-off point. Suddenly the thought of heading into a city, when I would soon be surrounded by the urban chaos of New Haven, seemed far less appealing than a walk up in the hills.

After changing my train reservation, I boarded a bus heading up into the Rondane. I was the only passenger. This did not surprise me, since the road was suicidally dangerous. If this driver as much as sneezed, we were both bound for glory. Clearing the tree line, the bus roared in a cloud of dust past a collection of huts. Grass and dandelions grew upon their turfed rooftops. Beyond the huts we emerged onto a plain of tundra, and the road ended in the middle of nowhere at a small parking lot called Spranget. That such a place should have a name seemed strange to me.

As soon as the driver opened the door, I scrambled off the bus. A sound of rushing water filled my ears. Above, the vault of the sky was unobstructed by the horizon and it seemed to me I could read in it the actual curvature of the Earth. I found myself at the beginning of a long path. It followed the course of a fast-running river that wound toward the distant round-topped mountains. Their snow-capped tops radiated the sun's light across the tundra's greens and browns. At the foot of the hills was a lake so perfectly sapphire that it appeared to be made not of water but the jewel itself. By the edge of that lake stood a fairy-tale house, dwarfed at the foot of a mountain called Storronden, which itself lay in the shadow of an even bigger mountain named Rondslottet. My ability to gauge distance was baffled by the lack of trees. I didn't know if it would only take me a few hours to get there, or the rest of the day.

This path, and the way it stretched toward the horizon, empty and without obstruction across ground whose merging colors glowed in this high-altitude light, had the appearance of a causeway between heaven and Earth. Its effect on me was similar to when I visited the Alhambra palace in Granada. I remembered seeing, on the walls of the mosque, an impossibly tangled ornamentation of design that instantly gave me a headache. I stayed and listened to the tour guide only because I thought it would be rude not to stay. He explained that my reaction was not uncommon, indeed not unintended. If you try to take it all in at once, you simply get dizzy. However, if you focus on just one part of the wall, you cannot see the whole. So it is, the Muslims believe, with the presence of God, which is too great, too overwhelming, to be grasped by the mind. All we can do is study the details, knowing that the whole is more than we can fathom.

I felt the same here in the Rondane. My first glimpse of the place had stunned me into a silence deeper than words. This was an old, old landscape, and my body and my mind responded to it with ancient instincts, sparked to life out of a slumber that was older than myself. Suddenly I felt so awake and so aware of everything around me, that it seemed as if the rest of my life had been spent sleeping.

WITHIN A WEEK, I had returned to the merciless early September heat of New Haven. I tried to forget about the summer, about the fishing boats and Norway, too. But time and again in the months and years that followed, bright pictures of my time in Norway would reappear, bursting like fireworks in my head. They were like what Robert Graves, in his World War I memoir *Goodbye to All That*, described as "caricatures." He would see himself at frozen moments in time—climbing from the trenches into No Man's Land or stuck in a Cairo brothel that had been converted into a school where he was teaching after the war. I would recall myself in places I had barely committed to memory at the time.

I became like Arneson, uncertain that I had actually seen the things I remembered. I wondered if those mountains were destined to become for me, as they had done for him, a place which remained forever beyond the horizon.

I knew I had to get back there someday, to understand what cast this spell on me.

In the meantime, I began to read about Norway, studying its history from the days of Viking raiding through the complicated periods of subjugation by Sweden and Denmark to its oil-rich present. In particular, I latched onto any books I could find by people who traveled in the same area I visited. Of these, there were only a few, and most long since out of print.

The earliest, titled *Through Norway with a Knapsack*, was written by W. Mattieu Williams and published in 1876. The most recent, *Walking Trips in Norway* by N. Tjernagel, came out in 1917. In between were the bizarrely-titled *Three in Norway by Two of Them*, (1882), *Norway—The Northern Playground* by W. C. Slingsby (1904), and *Rambles in Norway* by Harold Simpson (1912).

These travel memoirs, and their long-deceased authors, were to become my companions. Despite the relatively narrow band of time in which they traveled in Norway, they seemed not to have known of each other. Even if they had crossed paths, I was not sure they would have chosen to travel together. Although these men showed no signs of being reclusive, they were nevertheless loners. More precisely, perhaps, they were lone travelers. Traveling alone is an art form in itself. Anyone who has done this knows that the experience, particularly the inner world one inhabits on a solo voyage, is entirely different from one undertaken with companions.

I grouped these men under the general heading of "practical eccentrics." They certainly were eccentric, but they had to be in order to travel through the wilds of the Rondane, Jotunheimen, and Dovrefjell mountains, which form three separate but closely situated knots of mountains in the central part of the country. What is an eccentric anyway, but a person who has made a separate peace with the world? To make a separate peace, you have to walk a different path, which is what these travelers did.

As a result, they sometimes found themselves standing before people who had never seen a foreigner before. At other times, they hiked out of the trackless mountains and knocked on the doors of mountain huts, whose occupants had never received visitors of any nationality. It was their eccentricity that made the journeys possible.

I decided that I would see it as they had, at least as much as was possible with such an interval of time between my trip and theirs. This meant going alone and shunning the creature comforts of more popular tourist routes.

The solitary nature of my journey became apparent long before I set out. In my part of the world, to begin a conversation on Norway is to invite total silence. The country, and most everything to do with it, is simply not on people's radar.

I had really no idea what I was getting into. So far I had only seen the Rondane, and even "seeing" was too much of a claim. Until I returned, I had little more to go on than guidebook photos and litho-drawings that illustrated the older texts. The conclusion I reached from these memoirs was that illustrations, photographic or otherwise, would not be much use anyway. One trait these men shared more than any other was an inability to frame within the scaffolding of words the overwhelming impact the Norwegian mountain landscape had worked on them. It is not that they were unable to find the right words. The conclusion they reached, each in his own way, was that the words do not exist. Neither was it possible to do anything more than hint at it through pictures. In my first glimpse of the Rondane, I too had reached that same speechless conclusion.

Speechless or not, I decided to begin this second journey where I had begun the first—in Andalsnes, refuge of the deep-sea dreamers.

Chapter Two

The Great Silence

I AM STANDING ON THE PLATFORM AT OSLO'S SENTRALSTASJON, watching passengers board the dull red train bound for Andalsnes. Beyond the tracks, high-rise buildings clump against the skyline. Despite the dreary view, I am tempted to remain here and postpone my journey into the hills for a few more days.

I have many questions about Norway, its culture and its past, which can only be answered here in Oslo.

When I began reading about Norway, I rapidly became aware of how much I didn't know about the country. More disconcerting was that most of what I thought I knew was either wrong or misinterpreted.

For most people, Norway and everything to do with the country—its people, its history, its geography—represents an almost blank space in the mind. If you are an American, what you know about Norway, and you may as well lump in the rest of Scandinavia at the same time, probably centers around the fact that Vikings used to live here. You know about Vikings because there is a football team named after them. You think you know what a Viking looks like, because the symbol of this football team is a bearded Viking with horns coming out of his helmet. You know that the Vikings were a cruel and savage people, which is either appalling or very cool depending on your outlook. You might be able to back this up with memories of a cartoon strip about a Viking named "Hagar the Horrible." The football team is based in Minnesota, which you know has many immigrants from Norway. Other than that, unless you live there, you probably know as little about Minnesota as you do about Norway.

If you are British, you might know slightly more about the Vikings, since you were invaded by them, paid them vast amounts of money to leave you alone, and then were invaded again. And again. And again. Britain gave away so much of what became known as Dangeld, or "Danish money," that the country almost went bankrupt. In the year 1018, for example, they forked out 72,000 pounds of silver, with an additional 11,000 pounds paid by the city of London. In the end, even that wasn't enough. The result of these invasions is a good percentage of the people in Britain, in whose genetic make-up lies the bloodline of the Norseman.

The other thing most British people know is that Capt. Robert Falcon Scott died, along with several of his men, in an attempt to be the first to reach the South Pole in 1911. But what does this have to do with Norway? While Scott's death, which represents the absolute zenith of the British love of romantic failure, is known to almost everyone, it is nowhere near as widely known that a Norwegian, Roald Amundsen, beat Scott in the race, and neither he nor any of his men suffered as much as a case of frostbite along the way. For many people, there is something almost undignified in the way Amundsen ran away with the prize, compared to the noble suffering of Scott.

In both Britain and the United States, most people associate Norway with fjords, although they do not know exactly what a fjord is. They know that Norway is very cold and somewhere in the north, although not everyone can find it on a marked map.

It does not seem to matter that some of the details, like the fact that Vikings did not wear horns in their helmets, are wrong. The images are so engrained in our collective misunderstanding that it is almost impossible to correct them.

Beyond what little we know, or think we know, a great silence descends upon this land at the edge of the world.

I apologize to those people who know more than this about Norway. Clearly there are a considerable number who know a great deal more. In pointing out the general lack of knowledge, I am only showing where I started out myself.

I have emerged from my growing fascination with the place, as one often does, with more questions than answers. Many of the answers lie not on the glaciers or in the fjords, but out among the drab stone buildings of Oslo. There, the artifacts of history have been collected, and the truth about who the Norwegians were, and who they are now as a result, is revealed.

When I return here from my journey into the hills, there is much that I mean to set straight about the image I once had about these people and this place.

But for now, the lure of the mountains is stronger.

AS THE TRAIN ROLLS UP the Gudbrandsdal valley, what I see collides with what I have dreamed up from the books I've read. For months, and in some cases years, the many volumes have remained neatly filed inside my head. But now the pages tumble down like paper in a ticker tape parade, mixing the past with the present and the imagined with the real.

The first of these stories to be jostled from its shelf is Sigrid Undset's *Return to the Future* (1942). She once looked out, as I do now, on the peaceful waters of Lake Mjosa, but at a time when there was no peace in her life.

Undset is most famous for her medieval romance trilogy, *Kristin Lavransdatter*, and won the Nobel Prize for Literature in 1928. *Return to the Future* is an account of her escape from Norway after the Germans invaded on April 9, 1940. It is a harrowing story, which begins in Oslo, with the disbelief of those who first saw German bombers flying over the city.

Undset's flight took her along the same route as my train. At the time of her escape, its ever steepening mountains were still blanketed in snow. "In the heavenly spring weather," she wrote, "it was so difficult to understand that this was really the war.... The German invaders broke into a country which was entirely unprepared."

The disbelief soon turned to panic when it became clear that an invasion was not only under way, but that all attempts to prevent it would prove futile. After German paratroops took over the country's main airport at Fornebu, planeloads of soldiers began pouring into southern Norway. Despite losing more than a thousand men when the warship *Blucher* sank in the Oslofjord, German ships soon occupied all the major ports in Norway, and from these as many as three thousand men disembarked per day.

What resistance they met, in the form of the few available Norwegian soldiers and even some British troops, described by Undset as "more like boy scouts on an outing than like soldiers," were soon outgunned and overwhelmed by Wehrmacht General Pellengahr's 196th Division, who commandeered every truck, car, bicycle, and pair of skis they could find.

The "boy scouts" were part of the British 148th Brigade, under the command of Harold de Riemer Morgan, a hastily organized relief force sent to stem the tide of German progress.

By April 18, barely a week after the German invasion, Morgan's men had sailed into the harbor at Andalsnes. They were the southern element of a two-pronged attack designed to capture and hold the vital port of Trondheim from the rapidly advancing invaders. Andalsnes, which lies one hundred miles south of Trondheim, had been chosen because it stood at the end of the main rail line connecting the coast with Oslo. Grandly named "Sickleforce," Morgan's men were expected to swing north and link up with another British group, "Mauriceforce," which had landed at Namsos, eighty miles north of Trondheim, and together they would encircle the city.

Back then, Andalsnes was a sleepy fishing village, ill-equipped for the landing of thousands of soldiers. Nor were the soldiers themselves prepared for the fighting that lay ahead. The winter kit with which they had been issued, including the fifteen-pound fur-lined "Tropal" coat, rendered the men almost immobile. The commander of Mauriceforce, the one-eyed, one-handed General Carton de Wiart, described them as "paralyzed polar bears." Added to this, they had been issued with inaccurate maps, no radios, and no ammunition for their mortars. Half of their supplies were never unloaded. An accompanying contingent of French mountain troops, the formidable Chasseurs Alpins, arrived to find they had no bindings for their skis, rendering them useless.

No sooner had Morgan's men landed when they received a desperate message from the beleaguered Norwegian forces, under the command of General Ruge, falling back along the Gudbrandsdal valley. Ruge said his men could not hold out. If the British did not help them, German troops would cut off the British advance toward Trondheim. Morgan immediately issued new orders to Sickleforce and marched his men toward Lillehammer, arriving on April 21.

The sight of these troops filled General Ruge not with confidence but with dismay. His reaction was not unlike Undset's.

He likened them not to soldiers but to "untrained steel workers from the Midlands." They were mostly Territorials, reservists lacking skills not only in mountain warfare but even in the rudimentary application of their mortars or machine guns. Worst of all, they had no skis, with which they might at least have been able to flee efficiently.

The Germans advanced up both sides of Lake Mjosa and converged on the British troops in Lillehammer.

The British were completely routed. Within twenty-four hours, their fighting strength had been reduced from one thousand to three hundred. From that point onward, the men of Sickleforce were forced into a headlong retreat, which ended on May 2, when the survivors boarded ships in Andalsnes and headed home, leaving behind more than fourteen hundred killed, captured, or missing. Attempts to reinforce Morgan's men with an additional brigade of soldiers had only added to the death toll.

On June 9, General Ruge's last remaining troops laid down their arms and either surrendered or fled to Sweden.

Undset's own sons, Hans and Anders, were in the Norwegian Army. Anders fell while trying to bring a machine gun into position at the Segelstad bridge near Lillehammer. Undset's account is part rage, part grief, part savage propaganda. She finds herself comforted by reports of hundreds of German bodies lying in heaps by the side of the road. The Norwegian soldiers are all "quiet, well brought up, friendly boys," whereas the Germans are "not people, only some kind of loathsome animal.... Norwegian soldiers consider them repulsive vermin rather than people." Norwegian owners of houses occupied by German troops and later destroyed in the fighting "consoled themselves that it would have been impossible to have got their homes so clean as to rid them of the smell of Deutschtum."

I could not help comparing some of these passages to others that I had read as evidence of German racial hatred, rather than the hatred of those against whom the Germans were fighting.

With these thoughts swirling in my head, the world outside my train turns to black and white. Late summer colors are sheared away by winter. I see the fields covered with snow, banks of it drifted up against the low-roofed farmhouses. The leaning mountains are bearded white, waterfalls frozen into vast tongues of ice. Each bridge becomes a menace, to be blown into the rafters of the sky before the enemy can cross. Each building becomes a bunker, targeted by artillery and reduced to splinters, or booby-trapped for the enemy when they try to take refuge inside. I see the fields striped with the paths of skiers, and bodies of soldiers held up at the fences and gunned down by enfilading fire. I hear the hollow cough of mortars, the bestial roaring of tank engines, and the drone of planes overhead.

Forcing these grim scenes from my head, the colors pour back in—yellow fields of buttercups and warm blue sky, accompanied by the reassuring clatter of the train across the tracks. I watch the peaceful face of an old lady sitting across from me. She has fallen asleep on the shoulder of a tattooed and leather-clad giant who sits beside her, arms folded, staring into space, lost in daydreams of his own.

I change trains in Dombas and wander into town while I wait for the connection to Andalsnes. Dombas is a tidy little place, geared for the sight-seeing buses that pass through here on their way to the fjords. A giant rubber troll stands guard outside the tourist bureau, leering at a busload of Japanese travelers. Inside the gift shop, serenely patient saleswomen watch as shelves of Dale and Oleana sweaters are unfolded, held up, and then stuffed back into place. The saleswomen follow behind, methodically refolding the sweaters. The patterns and colors are all based on traditional Norwegian designs— vivid reds, blacks, and whites, or a blur of green, blue, and black in patterns which, from a short distance, look almost like the camouflage of a truckload of Norwegian soldiers who have pulled up at the café to grab a drink before heading on into a military training ground that my map tells me lies just north of here.

I wander over to a chart that illustrates the costumes, or bunad, of each region in Norway, and which are worn on special occasions, such as wedding days and Norway's National Day, May 17. The costumes are distinctively Norwegian, as are the color schemes, both of which find their origins in the peasant work clothes worn back when Norway was a colony of Denmark or of Sweden. It is the women's costumes that stand out. Some, like the black, red, green, and white horizontal striped dresses of the Setesdal region, are too garish for my eye, especially when topped by the blue, pink, and purple waistcoat and shieldlike baubled jewelry also required for this particular bunad. I prefer the simpler red-piped black skirt of the northern Ofoten region, and the simple clasps and tasseled black top that accompanies it. The bunad of the far north Troms region is even simpler, with a white-striped black apron and yellow brocaded vest. All the skirts are long, most to ankle length, and most of the ornate vests are worn over white shirts.

The colors of the chart begin to swim in front of my eyes and I go back outside.

On the veranda of the shop, I look down at a French tour bus that has just pulled in, its side emblazoned with the logo of a fishing expedition company from Dijon. The aging passengers pile off and make straight for the rest room, where they are stopped by a lockbox demanding five kroner, the best part of a dollar, for the opportunity to pee. The first one to arrive tugs in disbelief at the door. For a while the small crowd of fishermen seems utterly stumped, too appalled to act. Then one of them steps forward, holding out a coin. The door is opened, and the man who paid the money holds the door open, while the others file inside.

Before reboarding the bus, the men troop off to a kiosk where a sign exhorts all who see it to SMAKKER SOM BIFF! Beneath these words, a sun-faded flesh-pink hot dog lunges obscenely out of the sign. The sign itself is attached to the ground by a spring, causing it to wag back and forth in the breeze. As if this were not enough to put off one's appetite, three huge condom-shaped tubes hang from the ceiling of the kiosk, dispensing ketchup, mustard, or Thousand Island dressing.

I wonder what Undset would say of this place now. She spent some time in Dombas, on her way to the coast, and took refuge in the snowy forests at the outskirts of the town while German planes droned overhead. Some of these dropped incendiary bombs, which failed to go off and instead belched yellow smoke into the wintry sky. In between the raids, Undset watched disheartened British soldiers loitering in the streets.

Boarding the northbound train, I travel through the same tunnel where American military attaché Captain Losey was killed as he took cover from the air raids.

Within a few miles, we have passed beyond the Gudbrandsdal and on into the harsher landscape of the Romsdal valley. The Rauma River narrows into a frothing green and white torrent, like molten sea glass hurled along the stone-lined gully of the river bank. Through the open window, it roars above the engines of the train, which teeters back and forth along the narrow strip of land between the mountains and the water.

"It is ours," Undset wrote of this landscape. "No one has tried to wrest a living from this country except us.... We will not give up our right to it if we must wait a thousand years to get it." In 1940, when she penned the book, a thousand years might have seemed as long as it would take to prise the land from the grip of German occupation. But it is not the length of time that stays with me. Rather, it is the idea that making a living off the land should serve as proof of ownership. She begins her memoir by describing the stones that border almost every strip of cultivated land in Norway, evidence of how hard it must have been to clear the land for agriculture. "They are," she said, "silent witnesses of our right to this land which our forefathers for more than two thousand years have toiled to conquer so that homes for man could be built...."

The irony that these same forefathers soon ran out of farmable land and set sail to take by force the land no less hard won by those across the sea seems lost on Undset. "It was, in fact, by no means the whole people who rowed as Vikings, and the crews of Viking ships were farm boys." No doubt she saw a few farm boys among the frozen dead of both sides in the snow-covered fields.

The farther north I ride into the Romsdal, the harsher the topography becomes. The farms scraped out on these steep slopes are indeed triumphs of hard work and endurance, but they also show how small the hand of man appears against terrain like this.

I think about the places in which I have lived most of my life, at school in England, or along the shores of Narragansett Bay in Rhode Island, and, most recently, in starkest contrast to Norway, the condominium-blistered flatlands of central New Jersey. Nature exists in those places only when it manages somehow not to interfere with man's engineering of the world. But here the whole equation seems reversed.

I grow restless sitting in the comfort of this jostling train. I want to be up in the hills, where the stones are not cleared from the fields, where things grow without the consent of man, where no one can say, "It is ours."

I AM BACK IN ANDALSNES.

On my last visit, I could never have guessed that this town once thronged with my own countrymen, fleeing the scene of one of the more spectacular defeats of Britain's military history. When Undset arrived, the place was in ruins, the red glow of its burning houses visible far down the valley as Undset's car approached. I see a haunting echo of those flames in the reflection of sunset off the railway station windows.

Undset and I part company in Andalsnes, where she boarded a trawler bound for the northern port of Mo i Rana. After that, she made her way into neutral Sweden, across the Soviet Union, and eventually to America. From now on, my companions are of an earlier, more peaceful age, at least in this part of the world.

As I cross the narrow bridge that leads to the campsite, I try to orient myself with a photo of Andalsnes, which I found in Harold Simpson's book *Rambles in Norway*. Simpson stopped here on an extended boat journey along the coast. In that photo of the entire town, I counted only fifteen buildings (and one cow). Andalsnes has grown many times over since the days of Simpson's visit, but it is still a quiet place.

Although *Rambles in Norway* contains a picture of Andalsnes, there are none of Simpson himself. I am left to imagine this cruise-ship man, who seemed to spend more time arranging for transport than actually "rambling" anywhere. I see him standing at the rail of the ship, a little paunchy perhaps, with sturdy shoes and a Norfolk jacket, pipe jutting from his bulldog face and wearing a self-assured look that God is, after all, an Englishman. His opinion of the Norwegians is condescending in a way only a man with an empire would dare to be. For example, at the town of Moldoen, where he struggled to obtain a room for the night, he finds "no one in the hotel who could speak a word of English, and I had the greatest difficulty making my wants understood, even such an obvious and simple one as a room in which to sleep. This was hardly flattering to my hastily acquired smattering of the Norwegian language, on which I rather prided myself; but I prefer to think, not that my Norwegian was as bad as all that, but that the hotel people were particularly stupid."

Simpson no doubt resorted to the particularly British notion that the best way to communicate with foreigners was not to learn their language, but to speak English more loudly.

He is equally undiplomatic about Norwegian women. "Actual beauty is rare among them, but they are fresh-looking, well-built and not ungraceful, in spite of their slightly masculine element."

This is preposterous.

Either the ladies of Norway have undergone extraordinary changes since 1912, which I rather doubt, or Mr. Simpson needs to polish his bifocals.

As Simpson's boat entered the fjord at Andalsnes, the view took his breath away. "A wonderful pink light enveloped the snowcapped peaks, a deep rosy pink that gave to the mountains and the whole valley a strange air of mystery."

He had come here to see the Trollstigen, whose insanely winding path claws its way 2,800 feet up into the mountains at the head of the valley. The road was not built until 1936, leaving earlier tourists like Simpson at the mercy of horse-drawn carioles, who navigated the dusty roads not just along the valley but all the way back down the Romsdal. A daily car service to and from Otta was the only motorized transport, as the railway had not yet arrived. Simpson gloomily contemplated the effect of a train track through the valley. "Seeing that these facilities are what Norway, if she is to retain any permanent place among the nations, sadly needs, one cannot grumble at the prospect, however disastrous the result may be artistically."

THE CAMPSITE IS MUCH as I remembered—perched at the edge of the river, its water milky green with glacial sediment. Close to the camp store and shower room, several Winnebago-type campers seem to have settled in for the summer. I settle for a patch of ground right by the water and, dumping my tent out on the ground, try to remember how to set it up.

Pitching a tent is one of those skills I have to relearn every time I go camping. Assembling the enormous wobbly metal poles without poking your neighbor's eye out always takes a bit of practice. When the poles have finally been threaded through the color-coded sleeves in the tent, you then have, somehow, to bend them into the tidy bubble shape portrayed in the instructions. If there are two people, this is easier. One person gets inside the tent and holds it up from the inside, so the bending of the poles is less of an ordeal. But if you are camping alone, and not yet in the mood to beg for help, the procedure as you hop back and forth over the various poles gives onlookers the impression that you are insanely trying to reenact *Riverdance*.

Having succeeded in setting up the tent, I am applauded by an elderly Dutch couple. I reply with a dignified bow and, before they can start throwing pennies, make my way to the campsite commissariat.

The first thing I buy is a packet of crispbread, always good when hiking because it tastes stale right from the get-go and so you can eat it after it actually has gone stale and not notice. To go with this, I choose a tube of processed cheese flavored with smoked reindeer meat. It is the only kind they have left.

For the main meal, I have a choice of two kinds of stew. One is called Bogg. The other is called Sodd.

I am quite serious.

But how to choose? There does not appear to be much difference between Bogg and Sodd, except that Bogg sauce is darker than Sodd sauce. The serving suggestion on the label goes no further than suggesting I pour it into a bowl.

Surprisingly, Bogg turns out to be quite tasty, but bear in mind that I have been eating institutional meals off plastic trays at various boarding schools pretty much nonstop since the age of seven. I am acquainted with fried Spam, with chicken described by the Eton College dining hall as "vol or vent," squashed smoked fish called kippers, and Marmite.

One of the mysterious truths of eating while camping is that there are certain foods which you would not normally touch but which, inexplicably, taste delicious if eaten outdoors from a grubby mess tin while your eyes are stinging from camp stove smoke.

So it is with Bogg and Sodd.

As I squat on my haunches, spoon scraping the last Boggy-Bits from my mess tin, I gaze across the river at a farm on the other side. The bright red barn stands out like a drop of blood against the shelf of rock that rises almost vertically behind it. Beyond lies the mighty Romsdalshorn, a blunted snout rising five thousand feet above the valley floor. Against the enormity of this, I see the farmer himself, pitchfork over his shoulder, walking up a chalky road to the door of his barn. A sliver of black appears in the crimson wall, then vanishes again as he disappears inside. I find myself thinking of Thomas Gray's "Elegy in a Country Churchyard":

> The ploughman homeward
> weary plods
> And leaves the world to
> darkness and to me.

I think of the gentleness of landscape evoked by that poem. It is the kind I'm used to seeing from the train heading west out of London toward Swindon, where fields of rapeseed glow luminous yellow and the ancient Celtic carving of the Uffington horse still gallops across the green. I wonder what Gray would have had to say about these mountains.

Inside the tent, after a halfhearted effort to tidy up, I crawl into my sleeping bag and take stock of my traveling companions, or rather their books. After a hearty meal of Bogg, you are better off without human companions, and they are certainly better off without you.

I always travel with too many books. Of all the refinements I have made to my hiking gear, the inability to cut down the numbers of books I bring along has dogged me since the first time I shouldered a pack. The only real change these days is not in the weight or number, but the kind of books I bring along. I don't read much fiction anymore. I spend most of my days writing fiction and the last thing I can do at the end of a long day of fiction writing is to curl up with a good novel. It would be like jogging all day and then coming home and jogging.

I fall asleep reading Jerome K. Jerome's *Three Men in a Boat*, taking comfort in the un-ruggedness of Jerome, Harris, George, along with their dog Montmorency, and their misadventures on River Thames.

Inspired, no doubt, by the heart-stopping diet of Jerome and his pals, I wake up halfway through a dream of sitting in the Star Cafe, just off Oxford Street in London. In the dream, I am sitting among the cheerful red-and-white-checked tablecloths and old tin signs for Bovril, Gold Flake Tobacco, and Beecham's Powder. The Irish waitress, who has worked there as long as I've been going to the place, is bringing me a breakfast of eggs, bacon, sausages, tomatoes, and toast with marmalade. She is just setting the plate in front of me and asking if I want more tea. I open my mouth to say yes, and then I wake up drooling on my hiking boots, whose chunky sole is printed on the side of my face.

Sighing, I unzip the tent and stagger outside. My disappointment at being diddled out of a Star Cafe breakfast is lessened by the cloudless sky that fills my eyes. I make my way to the showers, allowing myself a moment of self-congratulation at having endured a night on the hard ground without crippling myself. When I was eighteen,

I spent two months hiking across the Ardennes and the Rhineland. I stayed in a tent every night, and when I reached home found that I could not sleep in a bed so I slept on the bare floor instead.

But now I am thirty-eight. Sleeping on the ground no longer holds the attraction it once did, but there is enough remaining of the romance of traveling with a pack on my back and only a tent between me and the stars that I am relieved I can still do this.

I greet the Dutch couple who applauded me yesterday as I was setting up my tent. Now they only stare, as if they don't remember who I am. I write this off as senility and proceed to greet everyone else I come across on my way to the showers, satisfied that I have retrieved all the vigor of my younger years.

I arrive at the showers to discover that the state of my hair makes me looks like a frightened muppet which, along with the boot print on my cheek, explains that odd look from the Dutch couple. Jamming a coin into the shower, I disappear in a lather of shampoo.

No more than one minute into this, at which point I am Michelin-manned with suds, the water cuts out. The machine has promised me three minutes of warm water, so I bash it with the heel of my palm, and it responds by spraying me with a deluge straight out of the nearest glacier.

I'm so flustered from the shower that I fail to notice I have not brought my toothpaste and accidentally squeeze processed cheese on my toothbrush and start brushing with that, which leaves me with reindeer-fresh breath to start the day.

Feeling thirty-eight again, and perhaps even a little older, I decide to take the bus to the top of Trollstigen pass instead of climbing it. From there, I plan to hike back down to Andalsnes, providing I don't run into any trolls along the way.

Chapter Three

Rainbows Like Wings

TROLLS ARE SERIOUS BUSINESS IN NORWAY.

On the one hand, they are great moneymakers. Like the one in Dombas, they stand six feet tall outside sweater shops: big-nosed, long-haired, snaggletoothed, and wearing grimy overalls. They hold up wooden clubs and grin stupidly at the tourists. But there is another kind of troll that does not take so kindly to such mockery. These creatures are heirs to one of the seven worlds of the Norse pagan religion, connected by the branches of the mighty World Tree, Yggdrasil. At its roots, three sinister women called the Norns spin out the threads of destiny for every living thing.

The trolls of the old faith only appear at night, since daylight turns them to stone. This is why so many landmarks are said to be the remains of trolls caught outside their caves when the sun rose above the mountains. They despise us, we Aesir who have life so easy, and have sworn to enslave us one day.

They are bunglers, too, undone by greed and clumsiness. My favorite troll story is by the Norwegians Peter Asbjornsen and Jorgen Moe, who in 1845 compiled a book of Norwegian ghost stories and folk legends (Norske Folke-Eventyr). The story is titled "The Boys Who Met the Trolls in the Hedal Woods." Two boys, lost in the forest of the Gudbrandsdal, come across three trolls stamping through the woods, lured by the scent of Christian blood. The trolls are as tall as the tops of the trees, and there doesn't seem to be much hope for the boys until they discover that these giant trolls have only one eye to share between the three of them. They pass it back and forth, one leading while the other two straggle behind. One of the boys gets hold of the eye, so that even though the trolls threaten the boys with all kinds of grief, the trolls can't actually find them. The boys ransom the eye for two pots of silver and gold and two steel bows for hunting, then return home rich to share the wealth with their parents.

Although trolls seem to pop up everywhere in Norwegian folklore, the land staked out on Earth for the trolls is a mountainous, sparsely populated region called the Trollheimen. It lies between the ports of Trondheim and Kristiansund, with Oppdal on its inland side. Crisscrossed by long and lonely paths, it is the province of reindeer, ptarmigan, and wolverine, as well as the long-haul hikers who march from hut to hut across its treeless valleys and through year-round drifts of snow.

The ancestors of modern Scandinavians had a feeling that they were not the first to inhabit this land. The trolls are the mythic remnants of these original people of the north, whose elusiveness fueled the stories that were told about them. Who or what they were, and what truth lies buried in the tales, is impossible to say. It's easy to laugh off these old bogeymen of legend when you are safe at home, but not quite so easy when you are in the wilderness, as afraid of being alone as you are of not being alone.

I DO WONDER IF LONELINESS might have been a better choice when I get a look at the driver of my bus. I have never seen a face less built for smiling than that of the man who plucks the ticket from my hand at the bus stop in Andalsnes. In his complexion and the deep-grooved creases that spiderwebs his face, he appears to be made more of stone than of flesh, like a troll who's half immune to daylight. He is also missing one of his thumbs, one of those injuries I can't help staring at and wondering how it happened.

Seeing only three other people on the bus, I reason that he has either scared off all the other travelers, or that this is some ghost bus that zooms unwitting tourists off to hell.

As we hurtle along the Romsdal valley, I take stock of these other passengers: a young couple with a spiky-haired son who can't sit still. They are dressed in purple track suits and speaking nervously in German as they rustle through a collection of chunky guidebooks. They look like a giant bunch of grapes left over from an old Fruit of the Loom ad.

What they must think of me, who cannot bear to throw away my precious hiking gear until it is not just old and frayed but disintegrating into subatomic particles, I do not want to know.

The road begins to climb, jackknifing eleven times, turning back upon itself like an oxbow river. The side of the bus swings wide over the cliff edges as the driver wrestles with the wheel.

The purple Germans have given up on their guidebooks and are now staring silently out the window. The woman's lips are moving but she's not making any sound. The man's index finger is pressed thoughtfully against his lips, as if remembering that he had planned to go to Holland, or some other flat place, instead of coming here.

And me, I am too amazed to be afraid. I crane my neck to see the tops of the mountains, which thrust from the Earth like daggers of rock. These mountains have names like "King," "Queen," and "Bishop," as if you are being led onto a gaming board for ice giants and will soon be one of its small and expendable pawns. It is an unearthly place, where water spouts from cracks in the stone and hunchbacked trees cling to ledges far above, defying gravity and explanation as to how they came to be there.

Now and then I catch sight of the old horse path, known as the Klovstien. Until the road came in, it was the only way across these mountains into the Sunmore valleys beyond. The Klovstien, which zigzags in the opposite direction from the road, is what I will be walking later, on my way back down into the valley.

My gaze is distracted by the driver's face in his rearview mirror. The more I see of his craggy chin, which seems cut from the same rock as the mountains, and his flat blue irises of the type Hemingway called "machine gunner's eyes," the less afraid I am. Because he is clearly not afraid. At this point, I don't care if he is a troll. He probably ought to be, since he must have the most dangerous bus route in the world, and no mere mortal could stand the pressure for long. But this man gives the impression of absolute disdain for any dangers we are facing. He has done this, I imagine, for as long as anyone can remember, and in his forceful heaving of the wheel from side to side, there is something of the Ancient Mariner in him, lost in his own private battle with the fates.

These musings are brought to an abrupt and unkind halt as the bus pulls out of its last mad curve and swings into a parking lot. In the middle of the lot is a long, squat building. It is some kind of café, and it is definitely closed. The driver swings open the door and barks, "Trollstigen Fjellstue." The way he says it, he expects us to get out, and there is no arguing with a man like this.

As the bus hauls off up the road, vanishing around a bend along which walls of snow rise taller than the vehicle itself, I look at the Germans and they look at me.

We are all of us suddenly conscious of being the only people for miles around.

Towering above us is the wicked-looking Trolltindane. From its summit is a thousand-meter vertical drop, the longest free fall in Europe. In 1980 parachutists leaped from the top and survived.

It is cold up here, and the German parents are wearing flip-flops. They are not going anywhere until the next bus comes along. Their son is only slightly better equipped, with puffy running shoes, which have little red lights in the soles. They flicker as he steps uneasily from foot to foot. A frigid wind flaps their baggy track suits around their legs, reminding me of the girl in Willy Wonka who turned into a blueberry and had to have the juices squeezed out of her. This is what she must have looked like after the Oompa Loompas were finished with her.

I wave goodbye to the Germans, who are huddling under the eaves of the closed café. Slowly, one after the other, they raise their hands and move them back and forth, like tired people polishing windows.

As I set out on the path down the mountain, the air is filled with the sound of wind careening down the narrow gullies and the roaring of the Stigfossen waterfall, which rushes under the road and spews out over a precipice, spreading rainbows like wings down to the valley below. I pause and stare at the place where the current bends over the ledge of rock. The force of its pale emerald current is both hypnotic and terrifying.

I am reminded of a story I once heard about some Arab emissaries who traveled to France sometime in the 1800s. They were brought to a huge waterfall—I forget where, maybe Gavarnie—where they remained as if in a trance, staring at the water as it cascaded down the mountainside.

Eventually, when the Arabs showed no sign of movement, their French guide began to grow nervous. He asked them what they were waiting for.

The Arabs turned to him in surprise. "We are waiting," they said, "for you to turn off the water."

The notion that the water could surge over the fall like this indefinitely had not entered into the heads of these men of the desert, who fought and died over muddy wells which dotted their kingdom of sand. They believed they were simply witnessing a show of Gallic extravagance.

I can't help feeling some of the same amazement now, but there is something else here, too. It rises above the noise of the water and is at the same time an aspect of silence. Simpson felt it, too, when looking out from the veranda of the Andalsnes Grand Hotel: "A remarkable silence covered everything, a palpitating living silence through which mysterious voices seemed to be speaking softly to one another. Is it Ibsen who speaks of 'a silence that can be heard?' If so, he must have been thinking of some such night as this in his own beloved country of Norway."

It is all around me now, but what I sense of it is less heard than it is felt. Something similar occurred to me on my visit to the Rondane, when I sensed that vague but exhilarating sharpening of instincts. Now I am conscious of something more specific, but no less challenging to explain.

It is as if some other, unnamed sense inside me has detected a vibration in the air. This vibration seems to be alive, almost sentient, as aware of me as I am of it. It is not a feeling of being watched. Not a feeling of being in danger. It is, perhaps, the awareness of knowing that something is out there beyond the limit of my senses. Or almost beyond. Somehow, being here has stretched the boundaries of my ability to perceive what is around me.

Continuing on down the path, I am filled with the exhilaration that can only come from making a journey on foot. I am glad to have my tent waiting for me at the far end of the valley, and a fast-running river to walk beside. A line from Francis Yeats-Brown's warrior-poet classic, "Lives of a Bengal Lancer," echoes in the back of my head:

"When there are no such camps and no excuse to hunt and wander, what will this world be like?"

By the time I return to the valley below, down the twisting, ankle-jarring Klovstien path, my senses have returned to their old margins. But the feeling that I was able to grasp something that until today I had not known was there to grasp remains tattooed on my brain. Now I understand what Simpson meant when he wrote, "There is no accounting for the effect that various places have on one's affections and one's nerves."

Perhaps the answer lies in where I am going rather than where I have been. Where I'm bound next, I will not see the ghosts of men like Simpson, but the ghost of my old self, waiting all these years at the gateway to the Rondane mountains.

LEAVING THE TRAIN AT OTTA, I pause to stare at the engine, whose red paint is tarred shiny black with dead bugs. But there is no time to dawdle. The bus is leaving, and in a few minutes I find myself once again hairpinning from bend to bend, as Otta grows smaller in the shadow of the valley below.

It is a small town, hedged between mountains and buried in their shadows except when the sun stands highest in the sky. The correct way of saying its name is not "Otta," as in "otter," but "Oota," as in what a Cockney says when he is insulting your nose. For disappointing pronunciation, it ranks with the Lofoten island village of Å, in the far north of the country. When I first saw Å on the map, I imagined it might be spoken almost like a sigh, as if admiring the sunset. In fact, Å is pronounced "o-wah," exactly the sound I used to make when, as a goalie in soccer, I regularly stopped the ball with my face.

This time I am the only passenger on the bus. The driver is a woman with green eyes and red hair fastened in a ponytail by a clip made of polished brass. She steers with one hand while she talks on a cell phone. Her voice is soft and sympathetic, as if someone is explaining some misfortune to her at the other end. She punctuates this other voice with a particular inward-breathing "Ya" that I hear in almost every Norwegian conversation.

In the distance I can see a curve in the Gudbrandsdal valley, beyond which is the site of a bloody encounter. It took place in 1612, in what was known as the Kalmar War, when Christian IV, King of Norway and Denmark, was attempting to hold off a Swedish invasion of his country. A privateer named Colonel Ramsay, leading a group of Scottish mercenaries in the pay of Gustavus Adolphus of Sweden, landed at Veblungsnes, just up the Romsdalfjord from Andalsnes, and proceeded down the Gudbrandsdal generally smashing things up, burning houses, interfering with the ladies, and so on. Ramsay was stopped at Kringen by a group of farmers who unleashed an avalanche of rocks and logs and then rushed the mercenaries, killing all but one man, who escaped. The sixty kilted Highlanders who tried to surrender were slaughtered. Despite this Norwegian victory, it was not until 1905, after many years of confrontation between the two countries, that Norway finally achieved independence.

I find myself wondering where that one man could possibly have escaped to as the pine trees give way to bony trunks of white birch. Then even the birches are gone, and what remains is a vast and treeless expanse of tundra. The light is sharper here and more defined, as if your eyesight has suddenly improved.

The bus deposits me among a cluster of turf-roofed log buildings at a place called Mysusaeter. I remember it only vaguely from my last time here, as my bus roared through on its way to the parking lot at Spranget. Only one bus a day travels as far as Spranget, and this is not it, so off I get.

A saeter is an upland grazing area, where cattle roam in summertime. The saeter fields are often set at such an angle that young children were sometimes tethered to trees to stop them from rolling away downhill. The responsibility for managing the summer farms traditionally fell to the eldest daughter, who would live alone, or perhaps with another sister, milking the cows, tending the goats, and making cheese until the autumn. The milk would sometimes be ferried thousands of feet down to the main farm by means of a cable, known as the Jern Streng.

Not all saeter communities are used for farming anymore. Some, as seems to be the case with Mysusaeter, have taken on another sacred obligation—that of the weekend hytte.

The word hytte can too-simply be translated as "hut," but it holds a more vaulted status in Norway than the English word implies. A quarter of the population own such hytte. They are usually buried in the forest or up above the treeline, and offer Norwegians a place of escape from their lives down in the valleys. Sometimes the huts are located so close to the main residence that it doesn't seem to make sense that someone would abandon the comforts of home for a woodstove-heated, out-housed cabin. But that is exactly the point. This change of gears toward a simpler life, where tasks like boiling water on the woodstove or chopping wood with an ax, that might take only minutes with the help of more advanced technology, may fill the day in your wilderness retreat.

These places are sacred to their owners, because they make a balance of the old world and the new. On these cabins in Mysusaeter depend the sanity of many people down in Otta.

The only comparison I can think of in Britain is the hut at the bottom of the garden, where a chap can sit and smoke his pipe, drink tea from an old tin mug, and read the paper among the rakes and trowels of his Victory Garden.

In northern Maine, where I live for part of the year, many people have cabins tucked away in the woods, some reachable only by boat or on foot, where they can hide away. There, as here in Norway, you can find people who are unable to make the transition completely. Evidence of this are the satellite dishes jutting like giant mushrooms from the otherwise rustic dwellings. Even bigger cheats, I have read in a strange little book called How to Understand and Use a Norwegian, conceal "phones in hollowed-out books, fax machines in old wooden chests and electric razors inside cans of ski wax."

The center of Mysusaeter is marked by a small shop and a phone booth. The whole village—and even the word "village" makes it seem larger than it is—appears deserted except for a welcoming committee of sheep, their wool dreadlocked with mud and burrs, who amble over and nibble at my pack straps.

I didn't have time to buy food in Otta and there is a handwritten sign in the shop window. I have no idea whether it reads "Back shortly" or, as I once saw in the window of a recently closed ice-cream shop in New Jersey, "To Hell with All of You."

I decide to wait and see if the shop will open anytime soon. Stretching out on the ground with my pack for a pillow, I watch the dandelions swaying back and forth on the turf roofs, like fans at a concert of wind blowing down from the mountains.

When I wake a short while later, I have no idea where I am. Why am I lying in the road? And why is a sheep eating my shoelaces? It takes me a moment to recall, and in that time a rust-fendered car has come to a dusty halt outside the shop. A woman dashes out of the car and into the shop. A moment later, a sign reading APENT is thrust into the window.

The woman has blue eyes, a pale, freckled face, and hair the color of polished mahogany. I have seen several people with her hair color since I arrived. It's dangerous, of course, to start making generalizations, and I certainly don't want to start sounding like Simpson, but on the whole it seems to me that there is such a thing as a

Norwegian type, if comparing them to their cousins, the Swedes and the Danes. The Danes are finer-boned, more likely to be thin and tall and blonde. The Swedes are rounder in the face and in their eyes, whereas the Norwegians are more likely to be darker-haired than either the Swedes or the Danes. Their faces are broad and strong-boned, their eyes deeper set. They are more rugged-looking than the other Scandinavians. You don't have to look far to find exceptions to these classic types, but I think they do make up a recognizable portion of the population.

The woman smiles and says, "Hey," the standard Norwegian greeting.

I "Hey" back, but then she says a whole sentence and I am forced to explain, in English, that I have no idea what she is saying. I feel like a fraud, and I see a change in the focus of her eyes. I am a stranger, and even if I am no less welcome, I am still a stranger.

I am annoyed at myself that I did not learn Norwegian. I tried to take it at university, but the only Scandinavian language on offer during my stay at Yale was a course in intermediate Swedish. I suppose I could have tried to learn it on my own, and right now, muttering helplessly in English, I wish I had.

It's not that we can't communicate. She, like almost every other Norwegian I have met, speaks very good English. It's just that I feel disrespectful somehow. The arrogance of English-speaking tourists, refusing to speak any language but their own and genuinely incredulous that the rest of the world cannot do so as well, is one of the great and lasting shames of the Anglo-Saxon world. That the Norwegians slip so effortlessly and unantagonistically into English only makes me feel worse.

On the one hand, it's not my fault that English is taught in all European schools but that not all European languages are taught in English-speaking schools. But it occurs to me, as I stand here among these sacred hytte hideaways, that the reason Norwegian culture and language might not have cast its net so wide across the globe is not because they couldn't but because they chose not to.

The shop is equipped with similar fare to the campsite commissariat in Andalsnes, which is to be expected because there are only certain kinds of food that can stand to be squashed into a rucksack and left there for several days while they are being hauled out across the tundra. I pick up a can of Sodd, because to have tried Bogg and not Sodd is only to have lived by halves. Also, on the woman's recommendation, I pick up something called Trondheim's Turistproviant. It comes in a smart off-white tin, the writing swirly and old-fashioned and flanked by those little gold badges, completely illegible, like you see on bottles of 4711 Cologne, which indicate a prize won in some ancient exposition. The product seems to have such faultless pedigree than I purchase several tins, along with the usual flatbread, a caramel-colored slab of Gjetost goat's cheese, and several bars of soberly packaged Freja chocolate.

Just as I am about to leave, I see her unpacking a box of funny-looking wooden cups. She sees me looking and holds one up. "Turcop," she says.

At first I think it is just some kind of tourist knickknack, the sort of thing that would end up filled with buttons or spare change, gathering dust on some rarely visited windowsill.

She seems to be reading my mind, because she grips it by its short, blunt handle and tilts it, as if taking a drink. "For use," she says. "Climbers in Norway have these. You let the water drip from ice branches. From there, it is safe to drink."

It takes me a second to understand that she is talking about icicles. I take the cup in my hand and feel the way the smooth, round underside fits into my palm, and how the stubby handle rests between my thumb and index finger. There is a hole drilled into the end of the handle, through which a leather cord is looped and tied.

She explains that there are different kinds of cups, the best ones made of birch that has been dried while the white bark is still on it, giving the wood underneath a shimmering finish. Some cups have rounded bottoms, for resting in the grass or on the dirt. Others have flattened undersides, for setting on a table. The most authentic cups, she says, are the ones made for using outside.

"In time," she rubs her palm against the side, "the wood is like a part of you."

A minute later, with a turcop tied to the outside of my pack and cans of Turistproviant clunking together on the inside, I head up the winding road into the Rondane. My entourage of Rasta sheep escort me to where the road grows steep and then flop down in the road, exhausted by their efforts.

I pass an old man sitting on a rough-hewn chair in front of his hut, gnarly hands resting on his knees. My friendly wave falters as he gives no sign of knowing I am there. The man's gaze is fixed on the horizon, as if he is waiting patiently for someone to bring him some news.

Setting out on foot, with the weight of a pack on my shoulders, brings back to me the memory of other journeys I made when I was younger, through America, Africa, Belgium, Germany, Italy, and through the mountains of the British Isles. Now, seeing that old man lost in thought, I have the odd sensation that he is no stranger but an image of myself, glimpsed in the future instead of in the past.

Cresting the ridge, I see the mountains whose names I have memorized since the last time I was here—Rondslottet, Storronden, and Svarthammern. Their peaks rise above a faint mist, as if emerging from the smoke of their own primordial creation. The greenish-white spackling of lichen that covers their slopes glows with a patina like old bronze.

A few cars are parked at Spranget. In a rusty Volvo wagon, two tired hikers are sleeping. Their muddy gear is laid out on the hood to dry. Beyond the parking lot, no cars are allowed on the trail that leads to the Rondvassbu lodge, which I saw on my last visit, nestling at the foot of Storronden mountain.

The path climbs up the right bank of the Store Ula River, leaving it far below. The sound of the river remains close, as if the path itself is made of rushing water. On the far bank is a stone shepherd's hut, marked on my map as the Krokutbekkhytta. Behind it is the kind of swampy ground that sucks things down beneath its tar-black water. Appropriately, it is named the Satansrivillen. Past the shepherd's hut, the rounded mountains bulge like the knuckles of a giant fist, but on my side of the river the ground slopes more gently toward a rounded peak called Fremre Illmanhoi.

The earth is coated with low-growing plants. Everywhere there are blueberries, darker and more tart than the dusty blue kind I pick on Sally Mountain back in Maine.

The mist covers and then uncovers the mountains, as if toying with my prospects for a climb. In a place like this, you have to decide that you will go out even if the weather turns bad. Once you have come all this way, there is nothing to do but put on a brave face and start climbing, or else sit in the shepherd's hut and hope you don't fall into Satan's bog when you step out to pee in the rain.

Just as I am beginning to feel as if I have the whole place to myself, I hear a rumbling behind me. I just manage to step off the path before being flattened by a dozen dogs. They trample past, all tied together, pulling something that looks like a Roman chariot. Holding the reins to this contraption is a girl in a green jacket. Her long blonde hair streams behind her, and she laughs at my surprise as she and the dogs disappear in the dust. I realize then that these dogs are being trained for winter sledding, and that I have not accidentally stumbled through some portal in time.

It takes a little over an hour to reach the Rondvassbu lodge. The building stands on a small spit of land, between the waters of Rondvatnet Lake and the steeply rising side of Storronden mountain. The structure is really a huge log cabin, with several outbuildings containing extra bunk rooms and showers. There is also a clothes-drying room, or *torkebu*. A glance inside it reveals a hanging forest of muddy clothes, quietly and pungently steaming in the saunalike air.

Sprawled on the grass by the edge of the lake are the owners of these fragrant bits and pieces: a troop of Danish high school kids who have just come off the mountain. They have dumped their packs against the wall of the hut. From each pack, dagger-toothed crampons hang like the beaver traps of Canadian voyageurs.

Inside, the Rondvassbu is spartan but cozy, with bare wood walls and simple furniture, as well as a dining room that overlooks the lake. There are several sitting rooms, whose walls are lined with cushioned benches. In the corner room stands a fireplace made of the same stones as the mountain, still patched with old blooms of lichen.

Despite the bareness of the place, it has everything a person would want either setting out into the hills or coming back. Just as important, the things you do not want to see are not there, either. There is no TV, no blaring radio music, no candy machines, no gambling arcade or one-armed bandit flashing its lights in the corner.

The Rondvassbu, and many other lodges like it, are run by Den Norske Turistforening, which also maintains the trails. The word *turist*, whose English translation of "tourist" suffers from almost entirely negative connotations, is endowed in Norwegian with a distinct nobility. A "turist" is someone who gets there on foot. Considering how far into the interior you have to hike to reach some of the DNT huts on my map, the word is entirely appropriate. Not all of them are staffed, but all are well-maintained, their cupboards stocked with food. When you arrive, you take what you need and pay for it in a cash box located in the hut. There aren't many places in the world where such an honor system could function, but in Norway it does, and as a result the DNT has flourished for well over a hundred years.

The smell from the Rondvassbu kitchen, of boiling potatoes and sizzling onions, reminds me of my grandmother's on a Sunday morning. I have to fight off the urge to rent a cabin and forgo the pleasures of Sodd. Reminding myself that I came here to camp, I settle for a cup of coffee before heading down into the valley to pitch my tent. Hands clamped around the steaming cup, I look out at the stream-spliced ground, trying to decide where to camp for the night.

My thoughts are interrupted by the slamming of the door.

A man stands shivering in the entranceway. He is wearing matching green waterproof jacket and trousers, and long gaiters that come up almost to his knees. On his small day pack, a well-worn wooden cup hangs from a leather strap.

He nods hello and begins some mournful proclamation in Norwegian.

Seeing that I do not understand him, he switches to English without missing a beat.

"I am a broken man!" he says. Then he points toward Storronden's peak. "Never again!" He goes on to explain how he climbed up through those same misty clouds I saw hopscotching back and forth across the peaks. The poor man emerged from one rain shower only to be deluged by another. "It would have been easier just to be rained on all the time."

"Did you make it to the top?" I asked.

"Of course!" he says, "but I was traveling with two women, and they beat me to the summit."

Rather than let him dwell on this, I ask how the weather is supposed to be tomorrow.

He shrugs. "You cannot ask that far ahead."

I PITCH MY TENT A RESPECTFUL distance from the other campers in the valley.

To judge from their equipment, all are Norwegian and I feel an attack of Gear-Envy coming on. It starts with their tents, which are the beautiful forest-green, red guy–lined type made by Fjallraven. They are also wearing the green four-pocket Fjallraven jackets, identifiable by the leather fox emblems on their arms. The only Norwegian gear I own is a pair of oilers made by Helly Hansen, which I wore out on the fishing boats and which still hangs, fish blood and diesel-spattered, at the back of my mother's garage in Narragansett.

The packs of these hikers all appear to be Bergans, also made in Norway. There is one rucksack in particular, a Bergans of the old gray canvas and leather type, which receives my undivided attention. It is not unlike my own 1930s vintage British Bergen, a metal-framed style of pack named after the west coast Norwegian port, whose other claim to fame is being one of the wettest places on Earth. My Bergen is tattered and may, for all I know, have crunched the spine of a British soldier on his brief visit to Norway in 1940. I cling to it only out of nostalgia for the other journeys it has made with me. One day, I know, it will fall apart completely and join the other relics of my travels, like the leaky old canteen I hung on a tree branch in the woods near Wahlerscheid in Belgium, or the broken-handled mess tin I buried in the dunes of Essaouira in Morocco.

My rucksack may be old, but at least it was made for mountaineering, unlike the gear I brought with me on my first camping trip. I was thirteen at the time, traveling with the Eton College Mountaineering

Club to Snowdonia, in north Wales. We camped at a throne-shaped mountain called Cader Idris, at the foot of which was a freezing cold lake, or tarn. Lacking anything approaching mountaineering gear, I wore my black Clark's Commando school shoes, borrowed a spoon and bowl from the dining hall, and carried my gear in a laundry bag. On the way up, I fell into a peat bog and my bowl rolled away down a hill. According to Welsh legend, anyone who sleeps on Cader Idris will wake up either blind, mad, or a poet. After spending the coldest night of my life in a wet sleeping bag, I felt lucky to wake up at all.

Nowadays, I am better equipped, but much of my equipment is still as outdated as my pack. Camp stoves have been a particular source of distress for me over the years. Most are too fiddly. Some are just lethal. One paraffin stove blew up in my face, burned off my eyebrows, and left me looking permanently astonished. Others require priming with flammable toothpaste-like gel. They have to be pumped full of air, which then has to be regulated every few seconds. One stove was so unreliable that I was forced to set the whole thing ablaze and then blow out the parts that I didn't want to continue burning.

The stove in which I place my greatest trust is a palm-sized Esbit Model 9, unchanged since it was introduced in the 1930s. You place a white fuel cube on the metal stove. You light the cube. You put your mess tin on the stove. It heats up a can of soup in about four minutes.

If the price of leather and canvas is a slightly heavier pack it is, for me, worth paying. As for the rest of my kit—Gore-Tex into my boots, Capilene under my shirt, tent, water purifier, etc.—I have genuflected to the modern world.

What I like about the lines of this Fjallraven and Bergans gear is that it manages to hark back to a more graceful age while still making use of modern materials.

Traveling with a rucksack may burden the body with a weightier load, but it frees the mind to wander along paths too often blocked by the burdens of the working day. It is not just about where one travels, but about how one travels, because a fundamental truth about travel of any kind is that it teaches you as much about the place you leave behind as it does about the place you are visiting. The greater your departure from the comforts of home, the less you take them for granted when you return.

In the lasting twilight of the Norwegian summer night, I go through the camper's ritual of squashing any mosquitoes that have sneaked inside the tent, unrolling my sleeping bag, rolling my trousers into a pillow, and squinting, bleary-eyed, at a book. Even though night does not bring darkness, still there is a quiet that settles on the landscape. The wind no longer strums at my tent lines. Even the stream, which rustles by only a few feet away, seems hushed by the late hour.

Through the gauze of my mosquito netting, I look up at Storronden, the mountain which long before sunset cast its shadow over this valley. Tonight I will climb it in my dreams. Tomorrow I will climb it for real.

Chapter Four

The Disguise of the Blue-Eyed Girl

I AM LOOKING AT MY MAP OF THE RONDANE.

It resembles one of those diagrams of the human body, made out of different layers of transparencies. One shows the muscles, one shows the veins, and another the internal organs. Most of the map is taken up by seemingly endless swirls of gradient lines, illustrating the rise and fall of the mountains. They look like fingerprints, in places gentle and widely spaced as on the north/south slope of Randen mountain. In other places, such as the east/west slope of Storronden, they are rudely crammed together, like the life rings of a slow-growing tree.

Glancing up from the map, I can see the faint scratch of a path up the mountain. A few fist-shaped clouds drag their shadows over the Earth, moving like ships across a transparent sea.

It is just past 7 a.m. when I zip up my tent and head out. Even at this early hour, there are already climbers ahead of me. I see the specks of their brightly colored anoraks inching up the side of the vast, treeless mountain.

I am wearing my Ventile canvas mountain trousers, an undershirt, a sweater, and a lightweight anorak. My day pack is loaded with two one-liter Nalgene bottles, a tin of dried fruit, crispbread, and a can of Turistproviant. Tied to the outside of the pack, my new wooden cup lolls back and forth on its cord.

That is the extent of my mountaineering equipment. In general, I steer clear of ascents requiring ropes, crampons, helmets, and ice axes. I am not so much a climber as a wanderer in high places, with few ambitions to be any place I can't reach in a pair of lug-soled boots.

The path begins right outside the entrance to the Rondvassbu hut. It is ridiculously steep. A sadist made this path. Worse. A Norwegian sadist. By the time I clear the first ridge, I am wearing only my undershirt above the waist and still burning up.

Ahead, the gradient is less steep, but it is all rock. It looks like a library of fossilized books, dumped on the side of the hill. The cairns that mark the way are dwarfed into invisibility by the world of stones around them.

The pain in my thighs and calves and in the small of my back soon becomes a generalized ache. The water I drink goes straight out through my pores. There is no respite. Even after two hours of climbing over the tilting, sliding, groaning StairMaster-from-hell of rocks, I still can't see the summit. Each time I come to the top of a ridge, there is another one in the distance. Steam rises from my arms. Sweat burns in my eyes. I have not seen any of the other climbers, whose brightly colored clothing I glimpsed from down in the valley. The mountains have swallowed them up.

Far below, gusts of wind stucco the water of Rondvatnet Lake, which stretches its long, narrow body toward the north, staring back the blue of the sky with a darker blue of its own.

Having drunk all the water in my Nalgene bottles, I have to search out places not reached by the sun, where dripping icicles fang each ledge of stone. From these I fill and drain my wooden cup. The birch wood seems to ripple, as if there are tiny fish swimming in the water. On the ridge above, I can make out several streams of water, which coat the mountain with glittering tassels. Where I stand now, somewhere beneath the jigsaw puzzle of rock, I hear the gurgle of a strong current. The more I listen to it, the stronger it seems to be getting, as if at any moment the water will come geysering out of every crack in the mountain.

I push on. My heart is thumping crazily, but my mind feels perfectly clear, almost serene, uncluttered in a way it almost never is when I am down below.

At last I reach a table of rock at the edge of a huge precipice. Storronden has no other slope. It just falls away into space, eventually reaching a glacier far below. Feeding from the glacier is a stream that widens into a silty lake, but how big it is, I cannot tell. A ridge cuts off toward the west, sheer on one side and sloping only slightly less murderously on the other, until it reaches a river and soon begins to climb again. A raw wind blows down from the north, rattling the zippers on my pack and molding my trousers to my legs. I put on my windproof and retreat behind a rock. Taking out my map, I see that this ridge is called the Rondvasshogdi and that the river below is the Illmanntjornin. The drop on the other side, as near as I can figure, is 670 meters. I remember reading somewhere that a human body falls at a maximum rate of about 119 miles per hour. This means that, allowing time for acceleration, it would take almost 30 seconds to reach the bottom.

The colors of this terrain are so subtle that it would be easy to dismiss the whole place as brownish gray or browny green. But look at it even for a few seconds, and the colors seem to multiply, as if seen through a kaleidoscope.

I think about the inadequacy of the black-and-white pictures I found in a book called *Happy Norway to You*, one of several bizarre publications I came across when preparing for my trip. It was published in 1949, and its cover shows a cartoonish series of mountains rising from an ice-white sea, on which a cutout photo of a couple stand wearing shorts and the kind of dainty sandals that wouldn't last five minutes in these hills.

The first photo inside shows a young woman in a bathing suit, washing herself in a stream. The camera stares right down her cleavage. This is an odd beginning. I mean, why is she washing herself? The caption that accompanies this only adds to the confusion. "Hello everybody!" it reads. "Just a moment, please, and I'll be ready to show you around this country. In the meantime you may as well have a little look at me."

"My God," I thought, "it's a vintage porn mag!"

I was already a little jumpy about this after an unfortunate Web site experience the day before. I had been searching for some information on the Norwegian explorer Amundsen when I noticed a site called "Norwegian Celebrities." Realizing that I did not know of many Norwegian celebrities, I clicked on it. The screen exploded into a maze of female body parts. Web site after Web site popped into view, as if someone were fanning a deck of naked-lady playing cards in front of my face. I should add that this was on a school computer in the faculty lounge of the Peddie campus, where I teach one class a week. Terrified that someone would look over my shoulder, I began to click them off, but as soon as I got rid of one, another appeared. At no point did I see anything to do with Norway. It seemed a very long time before the last of these sites disappeared, after which I felt obliged to turn myself in to the school tech department, before Peddie security decided to escort me from the premises. Several sarcastic comments later, I was released from the bleeping, buzzing, plastic-smelling tech room and added the episode to my far-from-empty file of embarrassing moments as a teacher.

The soapy lady in Happy Norway to You was a far cry from anything I had glimpsed on the computer, and she disappeared from the remainder of the book, which consisted mostly of dramatic Norwegian landscapes. Some of the pictures, like one of a man standing on a rock overlooking the Norheimsund gorge in the Haranguer mountains, were the stuff of Caspar Friedrich paintings. Others were more notable for their antique machinery, like the shot of Sandringham seaplanes belonging to the Norwegian Air Lines, long since amalgamated into the present-day SAS, as they flew above the Arctic Circle.

However spectacular the content, all of the pictures suffered from being black and white. Perhaps Ansel Adams could have pulled it off, with his huge negatives and insistence on red-filtering his photographs in order to provide maximum contrast. But even with those visual tools, the view I have now across the Illmanndalen valley would be nothing without the heathery colors that crowd into my eyes.

Remembering that I am hungry, I lay out a few flinty planks of crispbread and a squashed bag of nuts and raisins and open up the can of Turistproviant. Once my Swiss Army knife has inched around the edge, I glimpse a blotchy, flesh-colored mass of congealed fat and what I suspect is mashed garbanzo beans. Gouging out a clump, I try to spread it on the crispbread, but the stuff is too brittle and explodes into brown crumbs. After an adjustment of technique, I manage to assemble something like an open-faced sandwich. And it is not so bad, this ancient-award-winning goop. It is salty, and a little greasy, with an aftertaste something like cold split-pea and ham soup.

Cooled sweat clings like a sleeve of ice around my body, reminding me that I have to get moving again. Before I head back, I step as close as I dare to the edge of the precipice. The space beyond the cliff edge seems to hiss, not only with the wind as it races up the sheer rock wall, but with the emptiness itself. As far as I can see in all directions, there are only more mountains, more empty valleys, as if I have climbed beyond the rafters of the Earth and stand now on the frontier of a deserted planet.

Climbing down a mountain, my treacherous knees begin to act up. The left one has bothered me since the day at Eton when I dove to score a try and landed on top of another boy. Then a third boy landed on top of me, bending my left leg the wrong way at the knee. I heard a crackling sound at the time, but it was only a couple of days later that I discovered a loose piece of cartilage, which began to orbit my kneecap under the skin, occasionally locking my leg so that I could not bend it. For several months the act of walking downhill or even downstairs would bring the marble-shaped annoyance from its hiding place, but then the thing seemed to vanish. For years now it has left me alone. I keep waiting for it to reappear. One of these days I will have to go under the knife, but until then this bony satellite and I have made a truce.

It is evening by the time I get back to my tent. Sweat has dried powdery on my face. Daydreams of a hot bath and a cup of tea evaporate into the less cozy reality of hard ground and a sleeping bag. No tea, either. Brewing tea properly out in the middle of nowhere is such an involved process that even the thought of it seems ludicrous. And yet I recall the extraordinary steps my classmates would take to make sure they could have tea whenever the occasion demanded. I recall, on cadet exercises of the Eton College Officer Training Corps, seeing boys stooped like tramps over tiny stoves of World War One vintage, salvaged from the attics of great-grandfathers who had used these same stoves in the trenches of Flanders and the Somme. Balanced on these stoves were miniature kettles, into which carefully measured spoonfuls of tea would be placed once the water had boiled. They would even bring along flasks of milk and tins of sugar. Then, out in some muddy, rainy wood on Salisbury Plain, they would sit back against a tree and, sipping from a mess tin, reclaim the aura of civilization that was otherwise removed by camouflage clothing, green berets, and the weight of an FN automatic rifle. The pleasure it derived came more from the making of the tea than the tea itself, which usually had pine needles floating in it by the time the drink was made.

I sit outside my tent, scratching the dried salt from my face and watching the narrow, fast-running stream, whose bed of polished stones reminds me of a story I heard in Morocco, of the mosque of Abdel Krim whose floors were paved with the skulls of his enemies. This stream is one tiny thread of the Store Ula River, which runs beside the path from Spranget and empties out into the dark waters of Rondvatnet Lake.

A smell of cooking drifts over from the Rondvassbu lodge. I can see a few people straggling down off the mountain and heading into the lodge for a hot meal and a shower.

There will be no hot shower for me. Instead, there will be a very cold bath in that stream. If I just curl up in my sleeping bag, I will wake up tomorrow morning unable to move. I know this from the time when, at the age of ten, I went on a twenty-mile walk for charity that was sponsored by the Dragon School. It was not my bath night at the dormitory, and the matrons made no attempt to change the schedule. The following morning, my calves had seized up so badly that I had to walk downstairs backward, extra-fun when attempted on a staircase with five hundred other boys pouring out of morning assembly.

Leaving my clothes in a heap beside the tent, I step gingerly over the damp ground to the stream. There is no gentle way to do this, so I just jump in. The cold shocks the air out of my lungs. The speed of the current shoves me downstream, heels and bottom bouncing over the smooth rocks, until one hand grasps a gnarl of root and I haul myself back onto the bank. The first thing I see when I have squeezed the water from my eyes is Storronden, towering above me in a frozen avalanche of rock. Shreds of cloud trail like war-weary banners from its summit.

Afterward, I huddle in my sleeping bag, leaning out of the tent just far enough to tend the stove on which I cook a can of lapskaus, a chunky slurry of meat and potatoes and carrots, reminiscent of Dinty Moore stew.

I fall asleep that night to the sound of thunder in the distance, remembering how dreary it is to pack up a tent in the rain and hike out through a downpour.

I WAKE TO A SKY SO BLUE it seems all memory of rain has been forgotten.

After some cautious birdlike plodding around my tent, feeling my bones and muscles still intact, I load up my day pack and head out for the lodge at Bjornhollia. My route takes me along a path that skirts the steep slopes of Rondvasshogdi mountain on one side and the Illmanntjorning River on the other.

The track is narrow and muddy, better suited to sheep than humans. There are no trees in the valley, only windblown grass and rocks and gravelly slopes on either side, which would surely send anyone foolish enough to climb them swiftly back to the bottom of the valley, accompanied by a truckload of dirt.

The river pools, then narrows, then pools again, now clear, now brown, now soupy green, depending on what stream is feeding it from above. These feeder streams cut across the path, so that I sometimes have to cross them with a running jump that sends me tumbling into the heather on the other side. The river is loud, dampening the air and echoing back and forth between the narrow valley walls. But soon this sound fades into the background, and the place settles into a brooding silence.

Once again I am alone, although the lug marks of hiking boot soles from those who have passed by in both directions are clear in the peat-dark earth.

The only animals I encounter are ptarmigan, and the only reason I see them is because they decide to move. Their camouflage is perfect. The birds are a little larger than a pigeon, dappled green and brown like the lichen-crusted rocks among which they make their nests. They straggle off across the ground, slow moving and wings splayed as if wounded. But I know this is a trick. They are leading me away from their nest by pretending to be hurt. If I follow them, they will lead me down the path a ways, then explode into the air and vanish in a flurry of feathers.

Just before I reach Bjornhollia, I pass through a grove of white birch trees, bony trunks shimmering under their canopies of coin-shaped leaves, which patter with a sound like rain.

The hut, also owned and run by the Turistforening, is a smaller and older-looking version of the one at Rondvassbu. The wood is tarred black in traditional Norwegian fashion and consists of a series of low-roofed buildings looking in upon a central grassy area, where three knobbly-kneed goats patrol in search of dandelions.

I stumble upon several guests taking advantage of the sun. They lie stretched out on blankets on the grass, flip-flops on their feet and newspapers over their faces. At the sound of my footsteps, they sit up and stare at me. They look confused, as if they could not imagine where I have come from. I see none of the telltale muddy boots and hiking staffs that would indicate a group of mountaineers. Slowly, one after the other, they lie back down, square their shoulders against the earth, and fall asleep again.

The goats too have paused to inspect. One of them brazenly snubs me with an endless poo.

The old wood gives off a faint smell of tar, and heat haze shimmers from the grass-covered roofs. Inside the main hut, I see tables neatly set for dinner. From the dining room, there is a view down into a valley, where a lake the same blue as fountain pen ink lies fringed by pale and bristly swamp grass.

A tall woman appears from the kitchen, wiping her hands on a dish towel. Under her apron she wears a baby-blue dress with white fringe, like something Julie Andrews wore in The Sound of Music. Her eyes are the exact same color as the dress. They match so perfectly that her eyes seem to glow, and suddenly I do not want to go outside, do not want to hike all the way back to my tent by the Rondvassbu. I just want to stay here and stare at her eyes. She is the caretaker, she tells me, and asks if I will be staying for dinner.

I apologize, pointing back toward the path.

She nods and makes that inward-breathing "Ya" that, unlike all the umlauts, circumflexes, and rolling r's I have more or less mastered over the years, I cannot duplicate.

I buy a bottle of soda and a chocolate bar, then sit on a bench out in the courtyard. The goats line up in front of me, chewing and beady-eyed, like three punks sizing me up for a mugging.

For a while, the only sound is the rustle of newspaper, as a faint breeze twitches the face coverings of the sleeping guests. Then suddenly one of them sits up, as if woken by a nightmare. He stands and shakes his head, then scratches his full-moon belly and wanders into his hut, leaving the door open.

As I am leaving Bjornhollia, I pause to shut the gate that marks the boundary of the lodge and the path along the Illmandalen valley. I catch sight of the woman's face in the kitchen window. She is watching to make sure her goats do not escape. I raise one hand to wave goodbye. She smiles, and I turn back toward the path, those eyes still glowing in my head, as if I have been staring at the sun.

Two hours later, with Bjornhollia far behind me, a shelf of cloud appears from the south, sliding over the Indre Illmannshoi mountain like a pot being covered by a lid. The cheerful afternoon light disappears, replaced by gloomy shadows. The temperature drops. A storm rumbles like the echo of cannon fire.

I have fallen out of favor with the Thunder God.

Here and there, bolts of sunlight break like sword thrusts through the cloud. Then even they are gone. I can smell the dusty sweetness of approaching rain. Soon the first droplets fall, darkening the stones beside the path.

More thunder. Closer. As if the mountains just beyond my view are being shifted about like giant chess pieces. The Vikings believed that thunder and lightning were the result of the gods playing bowls with huge stones up on the white lawns of the clouds.

Ten minutes later, I am soaked. Impossibly soaked. Water squelching out of my boots. Rain in my underpants. Spitting the water off my lips as it runs down my face. This is not just weather. There is something malicious about it. I think about those people back at Bjornhollia, sitting down to their dinner beside the fire. In my half-drowned thoughts, they all change into trolls, shucking off their human disguises. The disguise of the blue-eyed girl, flesh and hair and dress all stitched together into one grotesque costume, falls in a heap to the floor. They tuck into the charred limbs of the goats, which are heaped on a giant platter on the table. I imagine I can hear the sound of their laughing, carried on the rain-sieved air.

The exertion of yesterday's climb is taking its toll. I stumble on the path, loudly cursing the clawing roots and slippery stones. To keep the rhythm in my stride, I begin to sing. The only songs I know by heart, and which are any use for keeping time, are hymns.

I made this annoying discovery when I was eighteen and hiking through Luxembourg. My memory of Luxembourg is that it was almost all mountains, and that the route I took was of a constantly rising gradient. Passing towns like Echternach and Ettelbruck, with their punishing hills and shoulderless roads, madly driven cars blasting by me with only inches to spare, I had to sing in order to keep myself moving. I was belting out "Men of Harlech" near a place called La-Roche-en-Ardenne, when the wing mirror of a Belgian camper whacked the canteen off the side of my pack and sent me sprawling in a ditch full of stinging nettles. I can't sing that hymn any more without clenching my fist, as I did at the fast-disappearing Winnebago.

The discovery was annoying because, in the nine years I spent going to compulsory chapel at school, I made no conscious effort to learn any of the hymns, but had sung them so many times that the lyrics became branded in my head.

I don't even like the words to "And Did Those Feet in Ancient Time," but the blasted song has a perfect cadence for tramping along the side of a road when your legs are about to collapse underneath you and only the overriding capacity of music can keep you going.

I also serenaded the grizzly bears in Glacier National Park in Montana with all the best of tuneful Christian virtue. But I sang then out of fear. I was ten miles in from the Going-to-the-Sun camping area when I saw the huge footprints of a bear that had crossed the path I was hiking. I spotted huge boulders, the likes of which I could not have budged without a forklift truck, tossed aside by grizzlies so that they could reach the mice and grubs that were hiding underneath. The week before, a jogger coming around a corner had run straight into a bear and did not survive the encounter.

When you get to Glacier National Park, you are expected to sit through a film that explains the various dangers you might face if hiking into the interior. It just feels unnecessary to be sitting in the visitor's center, wearing all your gear and watching a film when your body is itching to get out on the trail. However, by the time you have finished watching the film, even having gotten out of your car seems unnecessary. The underlying message behind the film, and of everything else I've learned about bear encounters, is that for every method you can use to deter a bear from pulling you to pieces, there are an equal number of exceptions to the rule.

The first thing you are supposed to do when you see a bear is stop. Don't run away. This would only trigger its pursuit response, and since a bear can run faster than a person, you are finished. Having stopped, you are then supposed to puff up your body to make yourself appear as big as possible, even turning sideways so the bear can see the bulk of your pack and think, perhaps, that you will be too much trouble to kill. If that doesn't work, the bear will probably charge you. It might only be a feint, and the bear might veer away at the last moment, but in any case you are supposed to curl up in a ball on the ground, head tucked in, and hope that after it has finished batting you around and clawing the pack off your back, it will get bored and leave you alone.

The best thing is to avoid an encounter at all. If the bear can hear you coming, it might get out of the way rather than wait to see who you are. For this purpose, you can buy bells to tie to your boot laces or around your ankles, making you feel vaguely like a Morris dancer as you jingle off into the woods.

And then, of course, there is the singing. I wonder how many hikers setting out into bear country come to the sudden and unpleasant realization that the only songs they know are "Kumbaya," "Ten Thousand Bottles of Beer on the Wall," and "Michael, Row the Boat Ashore."

My crooning to the bears would not be such a crime if I could actually sing, but I cannot. When I tried out for the Eton choir, which was not a voluntary procedure, I went into a little room where a teacher sat at a piano. "Shut the door," he said. Then he bonged on a piano key and told me to sing that note.

"Bong, bong, bong," I sang.

He stared at me. "Don't say 'bong,' you idiot. Say 'La.'"

"La. La. La."

"Are you even trying?"

"Yes, sir."

"Then get out of here!"

And that was it for me and the choir. Since then only the bears of Glacier Park have been made to suffer.

Now, sloshing past the swollen banks of the Illmanntjornin River, I wonder if there are bears in the Rondane. I know that bears have been seen in the nearby Jotunheimen mountains. But what kind of bears? And how many? I can't remember.

Over the thrashing of the rain, I begin to hear things. Several times I jump off the trail with a shout, convinced that something has sneaked up behind me. All the while I am barking out my songs of praises and even resorting to Christmas carols, so that I almost deserve to be eaten by a bear for being so atrociously out of season.

Arriving at my tent, I see raindrops hanging like glass beads from the guy lines. The flysheet sags with moisture. My mess tin, left out since this morning, is overflowing. I look around the waterlogged valley. The streams are full and frothing white. The other campers have fled, and the places where their tents once stood are now submerged. My own campsite is rapidly turning into a swamp. Even the Rondvassbu lodge looks deserted. The trail out to Mysusaeter disappears into the haze of falling rain.

I decide to leave. I will never get dry in the tent, and I can't get any wetter than I am right now. Somewhere in Mysusaeter must be a hotel. If not, then surely there will be a bus to take me back to Otta.

The contents of the tent are hastily crammed into my backpack, and the tent itself, sluicing water over my already drenched boots, is folded and then jammed into its various stuff sacks.

Only when I have clambered up onto the path do I look back. The outline of my tent's location is already fading into the earth. The peaks of Storronden, Rondslottet, and Storsmeden are all hidden in the mist, dissolved in the effervescing air.

As I head toward the parking lot at Spranget, it occurs to me that my hopes about hotels in Mysusaeter and buses to Otta at this time of day are the ravings of a lunatic. I don't have it in me to walk the twenty-odd kilometers down to Otta, at least not today, and I don't recall seeing anything other than huts in Mysusaeter. I realize I may be spending the night on the porch of somebody's weekend hut.

I console myself with the certainty that it will not be the most uncomfortable night I've spent. That prize must definitely go to the night I spent in the ruins of the Drachenfels castle, which overlooks the Rhine at Konigswinter. The Drachenfels was the home of Siegfried, dragon slayer of Wagnerian opera fame. What remains of his castle is so weather-beaten that it resembles one of those dribble-sand towers I made on the beach when I was a child. At the age of sixteen, as an exchange student in nearby Bad Godesberg, I had fallen in love with a young woman I met at one of the many formal parties I attended during my time at school. She had partnered me through the torturous rituals of *Francaistanzen* or what in England was called "Courtly Dancing." The half-term holiday after I had returned to school in England, I arranged to meet her for lunch in Cologne. Only someone who has been a sixteen-year-old boy at an all-male school can possibly understand why someone would travel all the way from England to Germany to take a girl out to lunch, with no expectation of anything other than lunch and the privilege of paying for it.

Having barely enough money to pay for the lunch, let alone the travel costs of getting to Cologne, I scraped together all I had and realized that I would have to arrive in the area the night before, camp in the woods, and then travel back the same day as the lunch.

I remembered having seen some dense woods near Konigswinter and made my way there in a rainstorm almost as vicious as the one that tumbles down upon me now. Arriving at Konigswinter after dark, the woods looked so dark and miserable that my courage failed me and I knew I could not stay there. Then I glimpsed the ruins of the Drachenfels rising up above the town and persuaded myself that there must be some shelter up there somewhere. An hour later, I was huddled up against a wall, flinching under the crash and boom of a lightning storm that would have inspired Wagner to write about the endless joyful carnage of Valhalla and the shrieking war-bitch Valkyries, if he had not already done so a century before.

The next morning, I unpacked a suit from my rucksack and dressed as I watched the sun come up over the Rhine. Then, still shivering from the night before, I bought the girl lunch and went home.

At first Mysusaeter fulfills my most gloomy predictions. I walk through the deserted village, head turning from side to side in the hopes of glimpsing some kind of public lodging. Every covered doorstep houses a sheep, none of whom seem inclined to share their digs.

But then, as I plod past the last of the huts, I see a hotel. It is not a small hotel, either. I don't know how I missed seeing it on my way up. It is the Rondane Hoyfjellshotell and Spa. A spa! I am saved! Simultaneously, I sigh with relief and shudder at the thought that I almost didn't come this far down the road. Instead, I came very close to spending the night with a sheep for a pillow. If I had woken up the next day to discover that I was sleeping a two-minute walk from a spa, I would not have seen the humor in it.

Outside the hotel, I straighten up a bit. Try to assume a jaunty air. Tuck in my shirt. Comb my hair. Eat a fluff-covered mint that I find in my pocket, realizing only after I have crunched it that the mint is in fact a piece of fuel tablet.

Entering the foyer, I can hear the splash of someone swimming in an indoor pool. In a room to my left, I see tables set for dinner. To the right, a couple in white bathrobes are drinking coffee. A woman, also in a bathrobe, appears from one room and disappears into another, leaving on the air a fragrance of lavender.

I, on the other hand, smell of Bogg and Sodd and sweat.

They will tell you to go away, says a headmasterly voice in my head. They will say there is no room available. They will stare as you walk dejectedly back into the hills.

Tensely, I fill out a form, trying not to smudge the paper with my wet hands and hoping that the receptionist can't hear the water dripping from my pack onto the flagstoned floor.

The receptionist busies herself with arranging the stapler, the telephone, the freshly sharpened pencils. She is wearing a gray jacket with a matching skirt. Her hair is neatly gathered in a ponytail. Her complexion is faultless, the kind you would only ever find at a spa in Scandinavia.

I hand over the completed form. "It will only be for one night," I say, trying not to sound pitiful but managing to anyway.

To my relief, she hands over a key. "Dinner is at six," she smiles, revealing perfect teeth.

With my composure sputtering like a faulty electric current, I thank her and head for my room. She has given me one of the cabins that adjoin the main hotel. Inside, the walls and furniture are bare pine. The place is immaculately clean. There are several beds, of which I immediately choose the largest. Setting my pack on the bathroom floor, I hot-shower myself lobster-red. Then I wrap myself in one of the fuzzy bathrobes provided and sit with my heels up on the radiator, staring out at the rain, which is still coming down hard.

Later that evening, as I dine on salmon in a dill and white wine sauce, I listen to the piano man playing softly in the corner of the room. Quietly, I recite the prayer of all who have come out of the mountains and find themselves in unexpected luxury: Oh, God, please don't let me wake up back in my tent.

Chapter Five

Cloudberries

IT IS STILL RAINING.

Fog wanders like the gauzy shrouds of ghosts among the huts of Mysusaeter.

I pick up the morning paper on my way into the breakfast room, feeling altogether civilized now and quite capable of meeting the gaze of the perfectly complexioned woman at the front desk. Turning straight to the meteorological section, my eyes grow round as I see dozens of jellyfish-shaped clouds, trailing their rainy tendrils down over the map of Scandinavia. Only in the western fjords is there even a rumor of sun. There, the international sign for partly cloudy, sun bordered by cloud like a badly broken egg, overlays the crumbly outline of the coast.

Fate and the weather have decreed that I will rendezvous again with Norfolk-jacketed and red-faced Harold Simpson (since this is how I have painted his portrait on the canvas in my head) at a place he found so beautiful it lay beyond his powers of description. It is the Geirangerfjord, one of the great unnumbered wonders of the world.

By lunchtime, I have passed through Otta on a bus bound for Geiranger. We cruise along the banks of the Ottavatnet River, where houses cluster on the narrow banks, with hills sloping steeply behind them. The people of this valley live in a world of verticals and horizontals. There is almost nothing in the middle. Their dreams must be filled with the rumbling of avalanches.

The bus stops in the town of Lom, whose wobbly road serves as an artery of travel from Oslo to the coast. In 1857, W. Mathieu Williams, author of *Through Norway with a Knapsack*, staggered into Lom after getting lost in the surrounding mountains. "Only those who have wandered alone over the trackless mountains can understand the painful feeling of having relied on a map and then finding it deceitful; it is like being jilted after a long and confident courtship." Based on my own experience, I would add that only those who are wandering alone can persuade themselves that it is the map's fault and not their own. Half starved, Williams flushed a ptarmigan and prepared to shoot it with his "pocket pistol." But then he looked up and saw that the bird was not as afraid of him as it was of an eagle, which was hovering above them both. Despite his hunger, he took pity on the ptarmigan. "To have shot it would have been like murdering a child, so I fired at the dark enemy above, and succeeded in frightening him away."

Having neither slept nor eaten in more than twenty-four hours, Williams reached the safety of the town but then collapsed. He awoke to find himself watched over by a "stout gentleman" who turned out to be the village priest.

Williams was an educated man, a Fellow of the Royal Astronomical Society as well as of the Royal College of Surgeons. He authored two other books, one called *The Fuel of the Sun*, which deals with "solar phenomenon and planetary meteorology." The other is a companion to Through Norway with a Knapsack, and is titled Through Norway with Ladies. It presents, according to the publisher's 1876 description, "the smoother aspects of Norwegian traveling experience as obtainable by those who do not desire to 'rough it.'"

Roughing it is something Williams seems to have embraced wholeheartedly in his knapsack journey, which took him from Oslo, then called Christiania, all the way up into Lapland. While passing through the area of my own travels, Williams elevated his slumming to an art form that leaves George Orwell in his Down and Out in Paris and London looking positively decadent. Williams's narrative is filled with helpful hints about washing shirts in streams and draping them on your pack to dry, as well as cautionary advice such as "experience has taught me that a muddy pedestrian ... arriving at a late hour is not always well received ... hotel keepers generally discover that all their rooms are engaged on the arrival of such a visitor." This obliged him to go from house to house. He sometimes found himself wandering around people's homes in the middle of the night, since no one locked their doors, with nothing to guide him but a lit match and the sound of snoring. More than once he discovered whole families sleeping naked ("in the costume of Paradise," as Williams put it) in piles of hay, from which he deduced that "nightshirts are not fashionable in these parts." With them, he shared the traditional evening meal of porridge, called Groet. This was served on a single shallow platter from which each person ate their fill, scooping up the gruel with wooden spoons. Afterward, coffee was drunk in the traditional manner, with a lump of sugar clamped in the back teeth. These Norwegians spoke the old Landsmal Norwegian, a coarser but purer dialect than the more formal Riksmal, which owes as much to Norway's former Danish masters as it does to the Norwegians themselves.

When no lodging was available, he slept in caves. One night, having crawled into one "shallow cavern," he put on all his clothes and curled up on a rock. Waking to find the place flooded, he managed to light a fire, which warmed him more in the labor it required than the flames it eventually produced.

Even back in the 1850s, most Englishmen in Norway were considered to be crazy. Williams mentions an Englishwoman, owner of a farm in Norway, who rode bareback and chopped wood in a silk nightgown. Another Englishman, this one an aristocrat, hired a steamboat to take him across a fjord so he would not have to be introduced to some other English people whom he wanted to avoid. Williams also heard of an old Brit who lived in a cabin and did nothing but hunt wolves and bears. Later travelers did little to dispel the Norwegians' opinion of all English people as insane. Despite their reputation, the English were treated with both curiosity and respect. When people discovered Williams was English, they immediately took off their hats, which for men in those days was a long red nightcap called a toplue, a fashion statement now reserved for garden gnomes.

I like Williams. I see him as a tall and jovial man, round-faced and sunburned, with a neatly trimmed mustache and clothes repaired with sturdy but unskilled needlework. Once again, I have no picture to go on, but this is the figure that rises from the yellowed pages of his book.

What I like most about Williams is the variety of his observations. On one page, he is exhorting the reader not to take alcohol along on a strenuous journey: "I have observed that in most cases where travelers have been found dead in the snow, an empty flask has also been found at their side." On another, he wants the whole world to be equipped with wicker backpacks that "combine lightness and coolness in a high degree." He even has a theory on why Norwegian coffee, "strong enough for a Turk," is better than the stuff in England. He attributes this to the fact that the Norwegians roast their beans in small batches in a frying pan just before they make the coffee. It is good for washing down flatbread, which he compares to "eating a hat box." The most remarkable thing of all is that he kept a price list, neatly recorded in the appendix, of everything he did and ate that cost him money. In this are entries like, "Milk–2 Skillings," "Boat, Man and Boy–20 Skillings," and "Mending Boots–16 Skillings."

Because Williams had something to say about everything, no matter what the topic, it is hard for me to imagine him setting out on a solitary journey. People like Williams need to share their thoughts as they occur, not set down in a journal to be retold later on. But Williams had something to say about this, too. "Even a congenial friend, however desirable in general traveling, interferes with the feelings and reflections which such overwhelming solitude and silence awaken." With thoughts like these, Williams struck at the core of what it means to be alone and on the road.

His words are so alive in my head that I half expect to see him as I walk now through the streets of Lom. Williams thought this town a "poor place" filled with "peasant farmers," who nonetheless impressed him with their kindness. "Norwegians," he wrote, "are remarkably polite, ceremoniously so in the matter of bowing."

Now Lom is a clean and bustling place, with no signs of poverty about it. The town is cut through its middle by a savagely fast-running section of the river, spanned now by a more modern bridge than the wooden slat arrangement Williams crossed on his way in.

At the bank, where I go to change drab green dollar bills for the more cheerful blues and reds of Norwegian kroner, I spy one small but telling detail of Scandinavian attention to the quality of life. It is a clip located just to the left of the teller's window. At first I can't tell what it's for, but then I see the old woman in front of me pause to set her walking stick into the clip, which holds it in place while she is writing out a check. Such apparently trivial inventions might not add up to much on their own, but I see them everywhere here—from the fold-out wooden seats in the airport elevators to the special children's wagon (barnewogn) on the trains—which seem to me to point toward a philosophy of life quite different from the one in which I live at home. It is so simple, and yet so fundamental, that one could be forgiven for not noticing it at all. But it is harder to ignore the statistics that place Norwegian standards of living among the highest in the world. Together with the superb levels of education, socialized health care, accommodation of the family (maternity or paternity leave in Norway is two years; in the United States it is six weeks), there is the overall honesty of the population, which I've not only seen for myself but have read about in all my books on Norway.

Being here has made me think about the degree to which people's outlook on life must be shaped by the landscape in which they live. What does it mean to live in the mountains? On the Kansas prairies? In the Sahara? And what does it do for the soul to live in a place where the landscape is entirely man-made, where what nature can be found exists only with the permission of man?

Williams met a Norwegian who had emigrated to the United States, but then emigrated back again. His reason was that he liked America but did not love it. Norway he loved but did not like. The love was stronger than the like, and how could it be otherwise?

A lot of people must love Lom as well, because it is the most crowded place I've seen so far. Wandering back through town, I pass a row of Harley "Fat Boy" motorcycles, owned by the most authentically Viking-looking men and women I have seen in flesh and blood. They are sitting at a café, watching tour buses bearing Czech, German, and Spanish license plates lumber in and out of town. From the packed campsite, only a few seconds' walk from the center of town, pours a constant stream of flip-flop-wearing children. They seem oblivious to any call of the natural beauty around them and instead are drawn like zombies to the various ice-cream shops along the main street. I cannot judge them too harshly, having been such a zombie myself in younger years, blind to the miracles of Niagara Falls, the Arc de Triomphe, and Buckingham Palace in a relentless quest to persuade my parents to buy me a Fudgesickle, a Berthillon glace, or just one more Cornetto.

Those not hypnotized by the siren call of sugar have come to view Lom's star attraction, which is so far removed from the modern conveniences of camping-supply store, supermarket and sweater shops that at first glance it seems to be like a mirage, appearing not only from another place but from another time as well.

It is a "stave" church, built in the mid-1100s and added to over the centuries, first in the 1600s to accommodate the stylistic demands of the Reformation, then again a hundred years later and most recently in the 1930s, emerging as it appears today. The walls of the church, composed of hundreds of vertical staves, are streaked with a coating of tar. The wood is simmering in the afternoon sun, and tombstones surround the church in a barricade of human bones. The additions to what must originally have been a tiny church jut out in all directions, seeming to replicate itself the way a growing crystal adds to its own shape. I count more than seventeen different sections of roof, all of which are tiled with pointed wooden shingles, giving the appearance of a giant iguana hide. Adding to this serpentlike image, elaborately carved dragon heads rear up from the roof itself, baring their teeth at every corner of the compass.

It is, by its design, half Christian church, half pagan temple, offering its original congregation a way to ease between the old gods and the new.

My first exposure to anything Norwegian was at a church named St. David in Wales. I remember going there as a young boy and seeing the ruins that, my grandmother explained, had been smashed and burned by Vikings in 1089. Before that, the church had been safe from raids, thanks to its not having a spire. These spires acted as beacons for Vikings based in Ireland—Finn Gaill as the Irish called them—spying the Welsh coastline from their oak-beamed longships.

Churches were the main repositories of wealth in these communities. What Christian would dare to rob a church when you have God as a security guard? The answer was those who had no time for a Christian God.

Things started to go wrong for the parishioners of St. David's when a visiting abbot ordered a spire to be built. The Vikings needed no more encouragement than this, and it wasn't long before their Drakkar warships ground up on the windswept beach of St. David's.

When the Welsh had finally had enough of these costly visits from the people they called y Kenedloed Duon, the Dark Heathen, they repaid Viking savagery with horrors of their own. I was told how they lay in wait for the Vikings, and once the warriors had gone inland for yet another raiding of the church, they came around behind the Norsemen and burned all but one of their ships. After attacking the Vikings, they flayed the backs of the men they had killed and nailed their hides to the doors of the church. Those who survived were allowed to go free, to spread the word of what was waiting for them if they came again. The Vikings took the hint, and their dragon-prowed ships never returned.

Whether this particular story is true or not, and it probably isn't, I could not hide a morbid fascination with these gangsters of the ancient world, who so terrified my ancestors that they used to pray Libera nos Domine, furore Normanorum—Deliver us, O Lord, from the fury of the Northmen.

The concept of one infallible god stood in sharp contrast to the dozens worshiped by the ancient Norse. The most popular of these was Thor, the red-haired, hammer-wielding god. He was forever getting into fights, either with Hymir, dark lord of the wintry seas, or Rungnir, the frost giant, or the hideous Midgard serpent. He even got into a brawl with Time herself, the ancient goddess Elle, who wrestled him down to his knees.

Thor was the workingman's god. He stood for strength and stubbornness and loyalty in the face of overwhelming odds, cracking the heads of his enemies with his magic hammer Mjolnir. Miniature replicas of Thor's hammer are still worn here for luck and is remembered on Thursdays—Thor's day—along with Tyr, god of war, on Tuesdays and Frey, god of fertility, on Fridays.

Despite the fact that Thor was the most popular, he was not the most powerful. It was Odin, the one-eyed, all-seeing lord of battle and intrigue, who ruled over all the world of Norse gods. He rode an eight-legged horse called Sleipnir, threw a spear named Gungnir, that never missed its mark, and carried two ravens on his shoulders. The birds would leave him every day, one flying west and the other to the east, circling the world and returning at sunset to whisper to him with their clacking coal-black beaks all that they had seen. Much as Odin knew, he was aware that he needed to know more. To remedy this, he traded one of his eyes with the frost giant Mimir, in exchange for a drink from Mimir's magic well, whose waters had the power of bestowing inner vision. To gain even greater power required a sacrifice, but as the highest of the gods, he had no one to whom he could offer a sacrifice except himself. So Odin sacrificed himself to himself, and hung his body from the tree of life Yggdrassil. For nine days he dangled there, thrashing in pain. The sticks that fell to the ground formed shapes which Odin recognized as the spelling of words, and in this way the alphabet of runes is said to have been created.

Odin was a fickle god, but in his fickleness, just as in Thor's short temper and heavy hand, the Norse saw their own failings and could accept them as part of the fabric of the universe, the burden of both gods and men.

To win over such a race to Christianity was no easy task, and Christianity did not come naturally to the Norse people. In the tenth century, King Olaf Trygvasson, an early convert to Christianity, ordered his people to be baptized, put to death, or exiled. Pagan temples were burned and Pagan priests blinded with hot iron pokers. A later Christian king, Olaf Haraldsson, was declared a saint when it was discovered that his hair and fingernails had continued to grow long after his death at the battle of Stikelstad in 1030.

From then on, all the kings of Norway declared their allegiance to Christianity, but the task of converting the pagan masses was far from finished. This work fell to missionaries, who often had to back up Bible stories with decidedly unchristian magic tricks in order to win over the followers of Odin, Thor, and Frey.

One story involved a monk who traveled with a huge cape, which he soaked in something like paraffin wax. He would announce that he would set fire to himself and that the spirit of the Lord would protect him. An assistant would set fire to the cape, and while the astonished crowd watched him disappear in fire and smoke, he would pull the cape around him and avoid being touched by the fire. Then he would emerge unscathed from the smoke, after which he apparently had no trouble finding converts.

This trick went wrong one day when he was ordered by a chieftain, who had figured out the mechanics of this stunt, to perform the trick again. Each wax coating only worked once and he was not given the time to paint on a second coat. The result must have been enough to un-convert most of his newfound flock.

The worship of one god may have simplified the ruling of the country, but it did not simplify the act of worship by the masses. So many saints required recognition that early Scandinavians created Rune Staffs, oval wooden rings marked with the symbols of various saints, as a way of marking time throughout the year. Early Christians could then keep track of the thirty-seven festival days considered important. Many of the symbols used are obscure, for example a fox to represent the baby Jesus on Christmas Day. Others are as clear as they are gruesome—a knife on August 24 to mark the feast of St. Bartholomew, who was crucified and skinned alive.

Although Christianity offered the people of the old Norse world some respite from the "savagery" of the pagan faith, it did so only after showing an ability to mete out equally appalling savagery of its own.

Despite the integration of Christianity into almost every aspect of daily life, worship of pagan gods continued for many years, particularly in Sweden. Stave churches like the one at Lom, and the equally spectacular churches at Borgund and Urnes, are acknowledgments of an uneasy truce between the Christian and the pagan faith.

I stand on line with the Harley bikers who have, after some loud debating, decided to visit the church. Their black leather gear burnished like armor and their helmets, which they carry in their hands, are not unlike the helmets of their ancestors, who might have stood in line here just as they do now, almost a thousand years ago.

On learning that there is an entrance fee, the bikers first try to persuade the woman at the door that she should look the other way. But she is having none of that, and the bikers stomp away, rolling their r's in a torrent of soft-spoken abuse. Walking into the antechapel, I can hear the muffled roar of Harley engines, like an amplified echo of the bikers' own purred swearing, as they thunder out of the parking lot.

But then I notice that one of them has not left. He is a tall man with a heavy chest and red beard. He looks just like the images of

Thor in the D'Aulaireses' book of *Norse Gods and Giants*, which I used to read as a child. At first I think something must be wrong with his bike, but then I see that he has changed his mind. With a determined stride, he makes his way back to the church.

The woman at the entrance has noticed too, but if there is worry in her mind, it does not show on her face. She wears a traditional Norwegian sweater and a long black skirt that reaches almost to the ground. She looks sublimely composed.

Thor arrives, leather creaking, leaving in his wake a scent of engine grease and old tobacco smoke. I wonder what he is going to say to this woman. I feel strangely detached, as if these people are specters of the two still-unreconciled halves of their country—the serene Christian and the volcanic Thunder God.

But there are no harsh words. Thor reaches into his pocket and squeezes two coins into the waiting hand of the attendant, as if squeezing moisture from his fingertips.

I do the same, and as I step into the church I understand the reason for her sweater. It is cold in here, and the air is filled with incense even though none is burning. Sandalwood has simmered here for so many hundreds of years that now the air is steeped in it.

The other surprise is how small the church appears inside. Rows of high-backed pews fan out in a cross-shaped pattern. The wood is plain and unpolished except by the rub of generations who have passed through here. The pulpit is an ornate cylinder just to the right of the nave. It looks like a big cookie jar, whose lid is suspended above the lectern. The altar is faced with a red cloth drape, on which a cross has been embroidered, and flanked on either side by a winged lion and an eagle.

The most unusual part of the church is the roof, which rises in tiers into the shadows of the ceiling. The bottom tier is ringed with the x-shaped crosses of St. Andrew, the next by tunnel arches, and what lies above that I can hardly make out, it is so cloaked in darkness.

Having walked the full length of the chapel, I turn to see Thor still standing by the entrance. He seems unwilling to come in. Instead, he just looks around, head rolling slowly as his pale blue eyes take it all in. There is something almost childlike in the way he stands, hands clasped loosely over his belt buckle.

To his right is a wooden cage, built around a row of pews. This was, I learn from the pamphlet, for prisoners to pay their dues toward the world above, while paying for their sins down here among their mortal judges.

On one of the pews, I see a row of small, neat cuts into the wood. Through each group of four is a diagonal slash, the old symbol for marking time in clusters of five. I count them and there are 129. One hundred and twenty-nine Sundays, if that is what they represent, shows the passage of more than two years. This graffiti strikes a discord, but not because it is graffiti. All churches are laced with it, including the Hagia Sofia in Constantinople, where the runes of a Viking named Halfdan, most likely a member of the feared Varangian guard, can still be seen upon the marble balustrade. The discord here is not in the marking of these simple wooden benches, but in the marking of time, because this place is so old that it seems to have been absolved by some greater force from the burden of growing any older. Everything in here, even the dust that twists lazily in beams of sunlight through the windows, is suspended in an unfathomable stillness.

When I look back, the red-haired biker is gone. Only the peaceful woman is there, fingers twined together on her desk in a strange mirror image of the biker's hands folded on his belt.

Across the road from the church is the Norsk Fjellmuseum, whose drab front conceals a beautiful interior. I am drawn at once to the cases of farm and fishing implements, which bear the marks of many years of careful use and repair—a world away from the disposable culture of the present. There is a particular patina that wood takes on when it has been handled over a long period of time. The sweat of use has polished the once-blonde pine of these fishing net handles, knife handles, and wooden cups, like larger versions of the Turcop that hangs from my pack. Each crease and dent is filled, like a scar in a human hand, until the wood itself seems to contain some life beyond its own existence as a tree. It is as if the combination of human touch and the weathering of the elements have combined to produce some other spark of life. I have seen this before, in my father's rock hammer, which chipped away at stones everywhere from Antarctica to Iceland. I see it in his old field boots, with their toes chafed to suede on the slopes of the Vattnajokull glacier and heels worn down upon the coral beaches of the Kerguelen Islands. It is in the old silver match case of my great-grandfather, and the pocket watch of my great-great-grandfather. And, of course, it is to be found in the traveler's gear of old rucksacks, mess tins, and walking sticks—anything, in fact, that bears the marks of long companionship and use. The students I teach back in New Jersey often wear their school baseball caps until they are so filthy and so ragged that I feel sure the caps will suddenly give up all pretense of solidity, turn to vapor, and drift like little clouds from the heads of their owners. But the cap itself is not important. It is the dirt that gives the pedigree of a veteran student.

The only possession of my own that seems to bear this kind of pedigree is a Parker 61 fountain pen, with which I wrote every paper in high school and which I still use in correspondence. It was always falling out of the chest pocket of my tailcoat as I ran to class and I kept expecting the pen to break, but it never did. Now I read the scratches on its barrel like a map of my own past, and my grip on the pen has left a permanent groove in the index finger of my right hand.

In another room, devoted to mountaineering, I am amazed to come across the notebooks of W. C. Slingsby, mountaineering expert and first to climb the daggerlike peak of Skagastolstind. There is even an ultra-rare first edition copy of his book *Norway, The Northern Playground*, published in Edinburgh in 1904. My own copy, which I was lucky to find even at the punishingly expensive price tag of $250, is a 1941 reprint. As if to mock me, it arrived with a sticker inside bearing the original price tag of thirty-five cents.

Of the handful of literary companions I have chosen for my journey, the only one whose face I did not have to imagine is Slingsby's. There is a photo of him in my book, taken at Skogadalsboen in 1908. He is sitting on a rickety-looking stool by an unlit fireplace, or *peis*, in a bare-floored and sparsely furnished room, still wearing his hobnailed mountain boots. Slingsby has an oval face with a high, bald crown, and a short-cropped mustache and beard. He looks a tough but kindly man, and reminds me of Robert Hardy playing Siegfried Farnon in *All Creatures Great and Small*.

Slingsby has become my hero, but he is also a hero to many Norwegians. He is credited with bringing the sport of mountaineering, as well as that of skiing, to the Norwegians. They knew well enough how to ski and climb their own mountains, but it was never considered a sport until Slingsby, and a very few others, began to leave their calling cards on the tops of Norway's fiercest mountains.

Not long after that, the Norwegians themselves became, and remain today, world-class experts in climbing. Evidence of this is the collection of ornate calling cards brought down from a cairn on the top of Store Knutsholstind around the turn of the twentieth century and now on display in the climbing room.

In the brief period before the sport of climbing caught on with the local population, these Englishmen were simply thought to be insane. There is even a printed quote in the museum—"Either he is quite mad, or he must be an Englishman." This was probably uttered by a man named Jo Tjostelsson, otherwise known as Jo Gjende, who, until the arrival of the English, was Lord of High Places in Norway. Gjende was a reindeer hunter, claiming more than six hundred kills by the age of forty-five. He even built a windmill on one of the Jotunheimen mountaintops to scare the reindeer down into the lower valleys, where they could more easily be stalked. But he quit hunting when he reached seventy-five, not because of old age but because, in his own words, "There is so much nuisance from people that the reindeer won't settle and all these Englishmen and city folk who go and climb at every opportunity. They are doing so much that it has become impossible for local people to go and hunt reindeer anymore."

Once Gjende had stepped out of the picture, men like Slingsby became elevated to almost royal status here in Norway. When Slingsby paid a visit to Oslo in 1921, eight years before his death at the age of eighty, he was received by King Haakon himself.

It wasn't just Norway who paid him tribute, but also the entire sport of mountaineering. Until Slingsby brought credibility to climbing in Norway, the sport had been snobbishly confined mostly to the French and Swiss Alps. By breaking this stranglehold, Slingsby placed a premium on the mountains themselves, rather than on the social stature of the climbing or "rambling" clubs whose members did most of the mountaineering. In doing so, he may have helped open the door for those expeditions to Mount Everest which, after several brave and failed attempts, was finally summited by Edmund Hillary in 1953.

Leaving the museum, I catch sight of another quote, which raises goose bumps on my arms. It is by the poet Olav Aukrust. "Forgotten is the old order," he wrote, "and that which the old people believed, sacred sites of the mountains, there where the unseen lived."

I am uncertain why these words have pierced me so. I feel as if it is not I who am in search of the answer as much as the answer itself is coming toward me, like some doppelgänger of myself, making its way down from the mountains, through the silvery groves that mark the boundary between the world of mountains and the world of men below.

Back on the bus, twisting and turning along the road that follows the path of the Breidals River, I hear an engine roar behind us. Looking back, I see the red-haired biker. He is overtaking us, shoulders hunched as he grips the handlebars. His red beard streams out on either side, as if his head is on fire underneath that helmet. With his helmet on, and goggles shielding his eyes, he appears to be wearing the same kind of helmet that was found at the Viking burial of Sutton Hoo. If his ancestors could walk back through the veils of time, they would, I know, soon trade their shaggy ponies for the Fat Boy he is riding now. And then he is gone, the sputtering howl of his engines lost around the next bend in the road as he races to rejoin his friends.

At the town of Grotli, the bus stops to pick up an elderly couple who turn out to be British. They are day-trippers from a cruise ship moored in the Geirangerfjord and both are dressed entirely in white.

As they board the bus, they are in the middle of an argument. The couple speak in such loud voices that the rest of us have no choice but to eavesdrop. The argument appears to center around whether they have been here before. Each landmark appears familiar to the woman, which the man, in his driving cap and cricket sweater, dismisses with various spluttering noises and the repeated motion of removing his cap and smoothing back hair he seems to have forgotten he no longer owns. Each time this happens—the pointing to a place, the assertion that they have been there, the spluttering, the smoothing— there is a tantalizing moment of silence, and the rest of us settle back in our seats, believing the worst to be over.

But then it starts up all over again. They seem only half aware of what they are arguing about, as if caught in a rhythm of perpetual dispute. Even at the point where it's clear that even they don't care that much whether they have been here before or not, they seem unwilling to give up the fight. There is something almost approaching tenderness in the perfect synchronization of their bickering. They never cut each other off in mid-sentence, do not shout, do not even seem angry. They are observing some protocol that has perhaps established itself without them even knowing. It is like watching a Ping-Pong game in which the opponents are perfectly matched and never tire.

When we reach Djupvasshytte, still several kilometers short of Geiranger, the old man announces, "Right, this is it," and hustles his wife off the bus, with what appears at first glance to be an inconsiderate harshness, but as I watch, I see how he takes her arm to help her down the steps. He does not squeeze her hand, does not rush her through the bits that her rickety legs find difficult. "You follow me this time," he commands. "Unlike some people, I know where I'm going."

The last I see of them, the old couple are wandering away across a construction site. At first, I can't understand where the old man thinks he is going, but then I realize that he must think we have arrived at Geiranger. I feel a shout building in my throat, to call them back and set them straight, but it is too late. They are too far away. I doubt it matters where they are. The only purpose of their trip to Norway has been to provide another subject for argument, and for their purposes, a construction site is as good as the Geirangerfjord.

For the rest of us, the Geirangerfjord is one of those places where the first glimpse carves itself forever on your brain. Later, as you sit in your car outside the shopping mall a world away, flipping through the pictures you've just picked up from the developer, you have to click your tongue with disappointment. Even if you did get it right, which if you are like me and paralyzed by most things mechanical, is not likely, the image of the Geirangerfjord will slip through the grasp of your lens. No picture image can capture it. Even the naked eye cannot absorb the phenomenon.

I climb aboard a small ferry in the fjord today, bound for the village of Hellesylt at the far end of the fjord. As the boat departs, I try to imagine myself on Simpson's steamer as it chuffed beside the sheer, dark walls of the thousand-foot Geiranger cliffs far back in 1911.

Along with a small handful of other passengers, I lounge on a bench in the sun. The echo of our engines bounces back off the rock walls as our bow cuts through water the color of molten sea glass. Waterfalls cascade from the rocks above, wreathing us in rainbows and making it rain from a clear blue sky.

As the fjord turns away to the left, we come in sight of the most famous waterfall, which is called the Seven Sisters. The sisters are actually a series of waterfalls that tumble from the same source and, by some fluke of stone, are split into what is usually seven wispy threads. These produce rainbows against the black rock of the cliffs. Today I count only six sisters. Simpson counted only four, and overheard a fellow passenger joking that he would demand a refund for false advertising. In fact, there are so many waterfalls besides the Seven Sisters that a veil of silvery mist seems to cloak the entire length of the fjord. Add to this the mighty stone formation called the Pulpit (Praekestol), the arcing bands of purple, red, and yellow in the hundred fragmented rainbows that seem to hover over the boat, and it is no wonder Simpson, and now I too, find words inadequate.

The inevitable downside of such beauty is that Geiranger's eleven miles of teal-green water is sliced by almost every cruise ship to travel the Hurtigrute, which is the name given to the path that connects Norwegian coastal towns by boat, from Bergen to Kirkenes on the Russian Arctic border. In places, graffiti has been painted just above the waterline, some of it even from the QE2. It seems a shame to allow these "Kilroy Was Here"s to remain daubed on the rock, much less to have done them in the first place. Perhaps, in a way, they are not much different from the ancient petroglyphs at Shipwreck Beach on the Hawaiian island of Lanai, which we now study and preserve, and which may have offended people a thousand years ago as these offend me now.

In 1905 an American traveler named S. G. Bayne passed through Norway on a whirlwind tour that included all the Scandinavian countries and a jaunt through Russia as well. His account of that journey, titled *Quicksteps through Scandinavia, with a Retreat from Moscow*, is as breathlessly told as the journey itself must have been. In those days, and still today, American tourists were noted for the speed with which they "did" the countries they had come to visit. Bayne's summary of the fjords is more telling of the man than of the place. "While the fjords are exceedingly beautiful," he wrote, "they have a typical similarity and, one might say, have become 'keel-worn' by the fleets of steamers that are constantly plying their surface. The average tourist at first sight becomes enthusiastic, then indifferent and finally 'throws up the sponge' and takes to smoking and reading French novels."

Bayne is right that there is an almost uncountable number of bays and fjords to be explored in this country. If the coast were straightened out and measured, it would stretch for over forty-five thousand kilometers. This jagged outline, when seen on the map, gives Norway the shape of a page torn roughly from a book.

But if the average tourist of 1905 became indifferent to this, then that average tourist was missing the point. These people Bayne encountered must have been engaged in checklist touring. They went to Chartres. They looked at it. Then they scurried off to the Parthenon. They looked at that. Next came the Leaning Tower of Pisa, the Acropolis, and so on. They came home with a million slides and claimed that they had seen the world. But they hadn't, in the same way that one cannot "see" all the paintings in the Louvre in a single day. You can look at them, but you cannot absorb them.

It is no less true for the Australian Outback, or the Erg Cherch desert in Morocco. These open spaces can drive people close to madness if they have formed in themselves a need to see one specific object after another, like the Eiffel Tower or the Washington Monument. The French even have a word for the melancholy that invades the soul in such seemingly empty places. They call it le *cafard*, and many a foreign legionnaire on outpost duty in the orange dunes of the Sahara fell prey to its unhinging power.

The trick is to develop an awareness of the space itself, and to see the poetry within it. Some people are afraid of large horizons. The Big Sky fills them with sadness and dread. These thousand fjords cannot fail to do the same, if the beholder does not learn to see them differently.

The real difference lies between the natural world and the man-made world. The man-made world fends off this so-called dreariness with the specificity of its buildings, its art, its carefully chosen color schemes, and the easy reach of creature comforts. If you take that sensibility out into the natural world, you will at very least be disappointed. At worst, you will go mad.

The solution, short of hiding behind the covers of a novel, is to learn to be still. There is an art to being still, even on the deck of a moving ship. What emerges is a kind of interior stillness that, if you are patient, comes upon you suddenly, like the breaking of a wave, as if you are being suddenly absorbed into everything around you. That is the real gift of a place like this, the full measure of which is uncapturable in words or pictures.

The cover of Bayne's book shows a man sprinting to catch a ferryboat that is just about to depart. His coat is undone and flaps behind him. In one hand is a hat box, in the other a suitcase and umbrella. The ferryman's arm is raised, as if to hurry him up. Behind him, the fjords and mountains and waterfalls are left unnoticed. The title itself, Quicksteps, assures the reader that nothing as fuzzy as "stillness" will be on the menu here.

At Hellesylt, I stop in at the Grand Hotel for a waffle doused in whipped cream and cloudberry jam, washed down with Gevalia coffee, a Swedish import that seems to be the brand of choice in Norway, too. Soon the waffle becomes just an excuse to eat cloudberry jam, which I spoon into the little waffle grids, glancing guiltily around the room to see if anyone is watching. But everyone else in the cozy dining room is doing the same thing. You kind of have to with cloudberry jam. Called multebaer in Norwegian, they are a golden color, like marmalade but with more of a glow. Cloudberries are late summer berries, whose white, cloverlike petals grow close to the ground in marshy areas. The berries themselves look like large orange-yellow raspberries and are used as an important source of vitamin C by the Laplanders, or Sami, as they call themselves.

The more jam I eat, the more curious I become about what these berries taste like before they are boiled up with sugar. When I have finally polished off the jam, under what I imagine to be the stern but forgiving eye of the waitress, I leave her a huge tip and begin my quest for fresh cloudberries. I find them, unappetizingly packed in unmarked plastic tubs at a fruit and vegetable shop in town. The lack of labeling is, the shop lady explains, a mark of authenticity. Fresh cloudberries do not travel well, and these have been gathered by locals, in buckets of water, up in the hills above town. They only come up for sale a couple of weeks a year. On the shop lady's recommendation, I buy a tub of sweet cream and a jar of honey to mix in with the berries.

Finding a secluded bench near the little factory where salmon are cut and smoked each season, I hurriedly pry off the tub lid. The berries form a sort of muted tangerine-colored tapioca. Cautiously, I stir the mess with my ancient metal spork and spoon some into my mouth.

I realize immediately how difficult it is to describe a food whose taste bears no resemblance to anything I have ever tried before. They are slightly musty-tasting, not sour like gooseberries or black currants, but not sweet like blueberries, either. Even though the individual components of their taste seem gentle, the overall taste is quite strong. The aftertaste is pleasant, almost smoky, hard to recall once it is washed away with a swig of water from my canteen. They are mysterious, and I feel as if I have been let in on a secret.

Then I pour cream and honey over the rest and stuff my face. The tartness of the berries forms a more perfect balance with the cream and honey than any raspberries or strawberries could do. The taste is miraculous. I eat it all, down to the last glossy nub of cloudberry, then sit back exhausted, fat, and happy.

Afterward, while waiting for the bus to Briksdal, I listen to the constant hissing roar of the waterfalls. It is everywhere, seeming to rise from the ground and tumble from the sky. Simpson remarked on this, on the verandas of the Union Hotel in Merok, which must lie somewhere on this fjord, but I cannot locate it on my map. There, as he listened to the tumult of a waterfall called the Storfos, he perceived, even over the noise, that very thing which eluded Mr. Bayne: "The broad bay, the wooden hills and the distant snowcapped peaks are all lapped into a wonderful stillness—a stillness that is hardly broken by the constant thunder of the waterfall in your ears, which from the very continuity of sound becomes in time almost imperceptible, and seems gradually to merge itself into the surrounding silence."

BRIKSDAL, WHERE THE Jostedalsbreen glacier reaches its icy fingers down into the green valleys below, is a major stop on the tourist trail. It is, more or less, on my circuitous route back toward the Jotunheimen mountains, and I have heard it is worth a look.

The road that bisects the luminously green valley is clogged with tour buses. I get a feeling in my gut that this is a bad idea but have been lulled by my visit to the Geiranger. I was expecting it to be mobbed, but it wasn't. Perhaps I just timed it right. But this, most definitely, I have timed wrong.

Everything comes to a standstill. A bus has broken down ahead. Our driver gets a call on the phone. A moment later, between forty and fifty elderly Japanese tourists pile onto our bus. The ladies are wearing high-heeled shoes and white gloves. I give away my seat and end up sitting on the floor while the tour guide, a Japanese man about my age, with a black leather jacket that comes down to his knees, stands over me, alternately apologizing to the Japanese and barking into a cell phone, presumably to get a back-up bus.

When we at last reach the café/bathroom/sweater shop that is the Briksdal tourist center, the bus is met by a small fleet of horsedrawn buggies. The Norwegian bus driver explains in broken English that the buggy passengers will have to walk a short distance when they get to the end of the trail, as the horses cannot pull up to the glacier itself. The man in the black leather jacket does not like the sound of this. He translates, taking much longer than the original message.

The tourists remain poker-faced, but the air in the bus becomes tense. As the passengers descend, the guide jabs some numbers into his cell phone and once again harangues the person at the other end.

Before I am even a few feet beyond the tourist center, the Japanese tourists are far ahead, lurching in their buggy seats, sheltered under brightly colored bamboo parasols, like giant versions of the kind you get in tropical drinks. The clip-clop of the horses fades away.

By the time I reach the glacier, the Japanese have already "seen" the glacier, returned by a different path to the bus, and are zooming away down the valley.

At a distance, the glacier itself looks like the wrinkled skin of an albino elephant, spilling down between a gully of rock. These wrinkles, dirtied along their knife edges, glow blue inside. It is as if they radiate their own light from deep beneath the ground. This blue shimmer is the result of tiny air bubbles trapped inside the ice. The bubbles have been subjected to such high pressure in the glacier that the gas is squeezed out, allowing only the blue spectrum of light to be reflected.

As I come closer, feeling a gathering chill in the air, I pass over beds of terminal moraine, the dusty grit of stones crushed by the relentless power of the glacier. The larger rocks are scarred in streaks, as if by giant cats with metal claws. This results from the glacier's dragging of one stone over another, in its slow-motion tidal wave down from the mountaintops.

These glaciers are constantly in motion, receding at the rate of a couple of inches a year in their reverse slow-motion flood, and yet they seem as permanent and ageless as the mountains themselves. The glacier is caught in a different ebb of time, like those giant red-woods that live five hundred years or more, in comparison with which our lives spin out with almost pointless brevity.

Impressive as the glacier is at Briksdal, it represents only a fragment of the Jostedalsbreen, which stretches for miles in an unbroken plateau of ice, so blinding white in the sun of a day like today that it would burn the sight out of anyone who did not wear dark goggles for protection.

Suddenly, I feel an almost overwhelming urge to climb this frozen stairway to the snow fields and leave behind the world of parasols and ponies. But my pack is at the bottom of the hill, and I am bound for the Jotunheimen mountains, on the trail of three Englishmen who fell grudgingly in love with the place, more than a hundred years ago.

Chapter Six

"I Am the Reason"

THERE ARE SOME GREAT TRAVEL GUIDES TO NORWAY, SUCH as the *Insight Guide Norway*, the *Rough Guide Norway*, Nortrabooks' *Mountain Hiking in Norway* and Cicerone Press's excellent *Walking in Norway* by Connie Roos. I enjoyed Andrew Stevenson's *Summer Light, A Walk Across Norway*, recently published by Lonely Planet, as well as several very old texts, most notably *Scandinavian Sketches*, published in 1835 and written by a Royal Naval officer named Lieutenant Breton. In 1861, F. M. Wyndham wrote a book about reindeer-stalking in this region, and Lt.-Col. J. R. Campbell compiled his travel notes into a book called *How To See Norway*. In addition, if you can find it, is Professor J. D. Forbes's *Norway and Its Glaciers*, published in 1851.

All in all, however, I was drawn to only a few travel memoirs. I fastened onto Slingsby, Tjernagel, Simpson, and Williams because the manner of their observations appealed to me. They were also, by and large, solitary travelers, or at least there was a certain endearing solitude in the manner of their writing.

There is one exception in this criteria of favorite books; the totally eccentric *Three in Norway by Two of Them*. Even the title is insane and, to judge from the book, the three men who lived the adventures that two of them went on to write about must have been Class-One Nut Jobs. Worse, they were English Nut Jobs. Still worse, they were Victorian English Nut Jobs, brightest stars in the Odd Behavior Hall of Fame. And finally, but perhaps not surprisingly, at least one of them was an old Etonian.

What does surprise me is that this book is available in almost every Norwegian bookshop, not only in its Norwegian translation but in the original English as well. The book is faithfully reprinted by the Norwegian firm of Andresen and Butenschon, and includes woodcut engravings done by the authors. It's a hefty book, some 350 pages long, and second only to Harold Simpson's in adding to the burden of my pack. But I never considered leaving it behind. It is, in all its outrageous pomposity, a genuine glimpse of an age now conjured into life by Merchant and Ivory films. While the men themselves have long since turned to dust, what drew them here, to the shores of Gjende Lake, remains almost unaltered since the summer of 1880, when they first arrived to hunt and fish and peer suspiciously down their long noses at all the Norwegians they encountered.

The heroes of the story are John, Esau and The Skipper, aka Charles Kennedy, James Lees, and W. J. Clutterbuck. The actual writers were Lees and Clutterbuck. While Leeds later turned his hand to lawyering, Clutterbuck remained a man with "no form of permanent employment." Kennedy is more of a mystery, and seems to have drifted into obscurity after deciding—horrors!—to get married. All three of them were, to quote the introduction, "gentlemen of independent means."

Standing now on the dock at Gjendesheim, at the far east corner of the lake, I can just see a stone house called Leirungsbue, where I believe the three men made one of their camps. The lake is long and narrow, bordered on its northern shore by a thin strip of level shoreline, which climbs sharply into vertical cliffs. The southern shore, while less severe in its angles, looks swampy and uninviting. Beyond, the rising ground is patched with glaciers.

Gjende is a popular destination, best known for its razor-thin Besseggen Ridge, across which over thirty thousand hikers pass each summer. In places, the ridge is only fifty meters wide, with a sheer drop of four hundred meters on either side. It was along this hair-raising path that the hero of Ibsen's *Peer Gynt* galloped on the back of a wild pig.

There are three stops on the lake, starting with Gjendesheim, then a lodge called Memurubu about halfway down the lake, and finally Gjendebu at the far end. Shuttling passengers back and forth is a ferry, at which Lees, Clutterbuck, and Co. would no doubt have raised complaint, since they had no such ease of transport for themselves. Instead, they brought along a contraption never seen before on the lake, and possibly never in Norway. It was a Canadian voyageur canoe that, on reaching the lake, they promptly filled with rocks and sank in knee-deep water. Strange as this seems, it is actually sound practice, since submerging the canoe allows its boards to swell and become watertight. It proved a worthy conveyance, despite the rough winds that occasionally ruffled the surface of the lake.

The best thing about this ferry service is not its transportation of people but of their packs. For a small fee, the ferry will drop off your rucksack at one of the stops along the way, and then allow you to continue on to the next stop, so that you do not have to lug your gear up and down the ridge. This service carries two blessings. First, a quick glance at the path leading out of Gjendesheim, which is the gentlest of the ridge routes, tells me it would be a wretched slog with a full rucksack. Second, because this is Norway, even though there is no one to guard your belongings, you can rest assured they will be safe.

I recently heard of an experiment in which wallets containing small amounts of money and the addresses of their owners were deliberately left in public places in various European countries. In each country, eight wallets were used. Only in Norway were all eight returned.

My plan is to hike the ridge starting at Gjendebu, making my way back to Gjendesheim. My pack will wait for me at Memurubu. There are no more than a handful of people onboard. All of us are driven inside by a cold breeze and spitting rain that races down on us from the far end of the lake. It does not bode well, but the weather changes quickly here, and none of the other hikers look deterred. The ferry travels close to the north bank, and, from where I sit, I cannot see the top of the ridge, only the wall of rock at its base.

At Memurubu, the ferryman ties a red label to my pack strap and heaves it onto the dock. It is the only one. I can't help a small flutter of anxiety as the ferry pulls away, and I watch my rucksack growing smaller, its red tag fluttering good-bye.

The rain has wandered off and, along with the other passengers, I make my way back up to the deck. One by one, we tilt our faces toward the sun, feeling the warmth on our skin.

When I open my eyes again, I half expect to see Lees, Kennedy, and Clutterbuck paddling about in their canoe. The woodcuts show them as thin, mustached, and garbed in heavy tweed, with Sherlock Holmes caps on their heads and long-stemmed pipes clenched in their teeth. These men lived to fish and hunt, and the book is filled with "ripping yarns" of trout brought in on the hook, of reindeer stalked among the rocks, and of various other animals, such as stoats, blasted simply because one of them had a habit of shooting at stoats. "Who can take any pleasure in life," they ask, "without a little sport to flavor it?"

Much like Jerome K. Jerome's Three Men in a Boat, whose real identities were also camouflaged behind assumed names, the three in Norway show each other little mercy when it comes to ribbing. There are various illustrations showing one man or another after an unsuccessful hunting trip. One portrays the bedraggled Skipper, as he "Returns to Camp Disgusted with Life." Rain drips from the end of his shotgun barrel, and his trousers are rolled up over the tops of his boots as he tramps through the mud. His expression is strained and fierce. Another shows John in his shirt and boots, with trousers slung over his arm, puffing contentedly on his pipe as he "Returns from Fishing in Summer Costume." My favorite is of the three men sitting around a table at the Rusvasoset hut. Their guns are racked on the wall behind them. A candle, jammed into an old beer bottle, burns on the table, and they are pouring themselves a drink "After a Day at Haircutting." Having myself been the recipient of haircuts-from-a-friend, I read into their raised eyebrows the same sense of astonishment that a person can be made to look so ridiculous, even with the best of intentions. It is as if each one of them is thinking: "I can't believe I have to look at these chaps for another three months. Perhaps, if I drink enough of this beer, my outlook will improve."

Excepting the beer and the fish they pulled put of the lake, they did not think much of Norwegian food. Of Norwegian cheese, they said, "If you eat it, your own dog will shun you. If you avoid it, you starve."

In the meantime, with the overwhelming hypocrisy only an Edwardian Englishman could fail to notice, they yearn for English anchovy paste. And even though they don't mention it by name, I know which kind it is, too. It is called Patum Pepperium and advertises itself as the "Gentleman's Relish." I expect it is the same now as it was back then. Although it now comes in plastic containers, it was sold until recently in heavy black and white china pots. A boy I knew at Eton practically lived off the stuff, and lined every flat surface of his room with empty Pepperium tubs. You eat it on buttered toast and if you do not spread it very thinly, you will gag on it. If you get it just right, toast the right temperature, butter perfectly melted, it is very good with a hot cup of tea. But for unappetizing color and texture and smell, it outranks even Turistproviant and, as I was about to discover, the Champion of Eye-Offending Food—Joika.

Scathing as they were of the food and of each other, the members of the Colony, as they called themselves, reserved a particular sharpness of language for the Norwegians.

They despaired of finding decent help among the locals, convinced that it was impossible to make them do more work, but entirely possible to make them do less. One woodcut shows a man named Ivar, a tramplike character in ratty clothes, whom the Colony hired as a cook. "Ivar is without doubt a perfect ass," they wrote, "and will never be able to do anything in the way of cookery, except perhaps boil a potato, and even in that enterprise we consider it would be six to four on the potato."

If the Colony men had traveled here today, they would certainly have given up Ivar in favor of a meal at the Gjendbu lodge. It nestles at the end of the lake, and serves as a last outpost for those setting out into the wilderness beyond. Here the valley forks around the Gjendetunga mountain, heading north along the Storadalen valley, down which the Storae river tumbles into Lake Gjende. The other fork heads south, over a lopsided bridge that looks as if it has seen the worst of some winter storms. Cattle graze on the Vesleae flatlands, which nudge up against the rising ground of the Langedalen. Beyond this, the forbidding glaciers of the Slettmark ridge scratch the clouds like coral raking at the hulls of passing boats. The passage through this wilderness is along the Vesladalen valley, reaching all the way to Lake Bygdin, which parallels Lake Gjende. They appear as two blue gashes on my map of swirling thumbprints, which mark the rise and fall of the Jotunheimen mountains.

The lodge is crowded with high school kids. Their socks hang from the windows like unraveled tongues. I stay only long enough to refill my canteen and grab a cup of coffee. In Norway, you are allowed to fetch a second cup once you have paid for the first. In the beginning, the coffee was too strong for me to sink two mugfuls at a time, but now I am getting in the habit of going back for more.

To climb the ridge up to the Memurutunga plateau, you have to double back along the lake. Before I have passed out of sight of the lodge, I come across a tiny cabin sunk into the earth. It has been left open, and serves as a memorial to an old woman who once lived here. There is a snapshot of her pinned to one of the beams inside. The photo is color, but I can't tell if it is one year old or thirty, and there is no date to help me. The woman seems ancient, her face as creased as my map of the mountains.

Her cabin is a rough-hewn place, with a sheepskin-covered bed, primitive table, and a three-legged stool cut from a single piece of wood, the branches making up the stool's legs. In addition, there is a fireplace and hearth, but not much room for anything else. Without windows, it is dark, even on a sunny day like this. The place seems cozy now, but I wonder if she stayed here in the winters, and what it must have been like to be shut in day after day, as anyone who wintered here must have been, going slowly mad like a character in a Jack London story of the Great White North. The Colony men had an equally gloomy appraisal of these huts. Near Gjendebu, they came across a "wretched little place … No Englishman would keep his dog in such a place unless it were dead."

Skirting the banks of the lake along a well-trodden path, I eventually find the place where I am to begin my climb. Here, the trail becomes like a ladder of rock, and I have to move hand over hand over the boulders. There are even chains bolted into the stone for pulling yourself up the rock face. As my hands sweat against the old iron links, I feel as if I am not merely struggling toward the ridge but locked in a competition against the mountain itself.

Beyond the wall of rock, a switchback trail leads so steeply up the side of the mountain that I do not want to turn around, for fear of getting vertigo. I am breathing hard but not exhausted. My body is growing used to this brutal regimen. My lungs no longer burn. I no longer drain my water bottle every five minutes.

The farther up I go, the less it seems like a competition with the mountain and more of a game against myself. Climbing these mountains places me as much in an internal landscape as it does in an external one. The feeling I have now, of hauling myself from rock to rock into the sky, is the same as when I sit down to write each day and scramble out across the tundra of my imagination.

Sometimes, when I am writing, I feel like the sorcerer's apprentice, dabbling with ideas which both frighten me and draw me in. They frighten me because I do not always know where they come from. They just appear, and I must follow them, out across this tundra. The farther in you go, the harder it is to come back. There is a point in the writing of each book when the world I have invented begins to seem more real than the world outside my head, and I spend more time with people who have been conjured out of thin air than with my family and friends.

When I was at school, I often could not fall asleep at night. I would find myself, long after lights out, with thoughts still rushing from one end of my brain to the other, like a school of fish caught in a net. All around me the other boys would be asleep, and their even breathing would fill the room with the rhythmic sighs.

In those long nights, I invented a game to pass the time. I would travel home in my thoughts, racing invisibly above the moonlit clouds, past airplanes whose passengers stared out into the darkness, past ocean liners far below on the snakeskin-rippled sea, past castaways on life rafts a thousand miles from land, until I reach the shores of America. I would decide on some spot on the map of Rhode Island, where I was living at the time. Sometimes it was Thames Street in Newport, where the wintry sound of sail cables rattling against sailboat masts made a crazy drumbeat in the dark. Or sometimes it was the old green metal bridge in Wickford, with javelins of icicles hanging from its cross beams. Or it would be the old gas station called Babbie's at the top of the hill, its pumps locked up for the night and all lights out except for the Coca-Cola machine, whose illuminated picture of a frosty soda can lay half buried in the snow.

From there, I would try to remember every footstep of the way home. Then I would creep inside my house and drift like a ghost through the hallways and bedrooms, seeing my brother and my parents sleeping in their beds. I drew my name in the frosted windowpanes and sat at the end of the dock, where black waves lapped at the barnacle-crusted pilings.

When sunrise bloodied the sky, I would fly away home, somewhere along the way crossing that deathlike boundary between the waking world and sleep.

I played this game so often that when I returned home for the holidays, nothing seemed real. Walking the beach, I once looked back to make sure my feet were actually making imprints in the sand. Another time, I reached into a rock pool and let a small crab pinch my finger, just so I would know from the pain that what I was seeing was real.

That is how it feels when you are lost out on the lonely terrain of your writing. But it is not always lonely. Often, when I sneak away into the world of stories, I have the sensation that I am trespassing. It seems less like the creation of another world than the visiting of a parallel universe, in which I know I am a stranger, walking the streets of an alien country like a man without a shadow.

I think about something Reinhold Messner, the first man to climb Everest without oxygen, said when asked why he climbed mountains. "There is no reason," he replied. "I am the reason."

I did not understand that until now.

Arriving at last on level ground, I look down on the lake and am surprised by huge blooms of white in the scarab green water. The white comes from silt washed out of the Knutsholet glacier, whose ice field spreads like an ivory sea into the distance.

Where are the thirty thousand hikers I have read about? Once again, I seem to have this whole ridge to myself. Following the path across the rock fields of the Memurutunga, I slide into the trance of my tapping walking stick. This trance is broken only by the wink of sun off the Langtjonne and the Grunnevatnet lakes that lie between me and the precipice, a thousand feet down to the lake below.

As I hike, I try to study the various shapes of the mountain, and to understand the subtle differences for which the Norwegian language has so many names. Like the Eskimo, with their multitude of descriptions for what English too-blandly call "ice," so the Norwegians, surrounded by so many peaks, have learned to differentiate between a cone-topped mountain (tind) and a round-top (ho). Then there is a jagged peak (piggen), as opposed to one that is steep on one side but gradual on the other (horn). If none of these will suit, there is always the general term for anonymous patches of rough ground (kampen).

On the banks of Sigurdtindjonne Lake, I find a sheltered spot behind a rock and sit down to eat my lunch. For several days now, I have been lugging around a can of stew called Joika. Its label is a cheerful red, but also sinister, like the color of hazardous waste containers. I cannot make head or tail of what is in it and bought the can because it was on the same shelf as Bogg and Sodd. There is a picture of something vaguely stewlike on the label, along with a cartoon Laplander in his traditional four-cornered hat.

I open the can and peer suspiciously at the brown sludge inside. By now I have learned not to judge the contents of a can by its color, or texture, or even by its smell. I'm not sure what remains to judge it by, except perhaps surviving the experience of eating it.

As I shake the Joika out of its can, I see that it consists of what appears to be gravy and meatballs. No attempt at vegetables here. Later, as it bubbles and plops in my mess tin, and the harsh white smoke of my Esbit fuel taints the air, I break out the crispbread and honey. Gnawing on slices of "hatbox," I gaze northward at the seemingly endless expanse of ice and rock that makes up the Jotunheimen. Some sixteen kilometers away, according to my map, is the Glitterheim hut. Other than that, travelers into that region are on their own. Step off the path, or lose your bearings, and you will wander out into the trackless terrain of the Nautgardoksle hills, or the ice-patched Trollsteinkvelven valley.

I am not surprised that the Englishmen preferred the valleys below. In the beginning of their stay, the landscape was judged less by its beauty than by its ability to yield up fish and birds and reindeer. They were hunters and fishermen, and the gleeful recounting of the slaughter of almost every animal they see is sometimes hard for me to read.

I would not have been good company for these killers of the Colony, although I used to enjoy fishing. I began by casting clamworm-baited hooks out into Narragansett Bay for flounder or bluefish. Later, I fly-fished the shallow streams of the Catskills up by Roscoe, using hooks with the barbs filed off and flies with names like Hairy Mary and Gray Ghost.

I have hunted, too, although without success. Once, having been invited on a goose hunt with two expert gunners out on the Eastern Shore of Maryland, I arrived at the starting point to find that we would not, as I had thought, be strolling across the stubble fields with our shotguns tucked under our arms, and for which I had dressed lightly. Instead, I discovered, we would be sitting in a wooden bunker at the edge of a swamp, waiting for the geese to gather around the decoys our guide had set out that morning. The other hunters had come equipped with thermal overalls, wooly hats, and gel packs that, when crumpled up, produced a pillow of warmth that most hunting buddies proceeded to stuff down their pants.

We arrived at the bunker soon after dawn. The marsh was blanketed in mist, with only the tallest bulrushes rising above the fog. We heard some geese, but by the time the mist had cleared they were all gone. This left us looking at a patch of dreary marsh and several decoy geese for the rest of the day.

Why we didn't simply arrive at three o'clock in the afternoon, an hour before the geese, I still have no idea. Sitting on the slippery boards of the bunker, I reached a state of coldness that bordered on delirium. At one point, when one of the other hunters retrieved a gel pack from some pongy recesses of his underclothes, pronounced it used up, and threw it out of the bunker, I waited a few minutes, said that nature beckoned, and went outside. I then found the gel pack and, casting all dignity aside, pressed its lukewarm smushiness against my face.

By the time the geese began to arrive, I was so frozen that I no longer cared whether we shot any geese. I just wanted to go home. But as the geese flew in, drawn by the quacking-honking noises made by our guide, I began to feel some vague killer instinct stirring inside me. Solemnly, I loaded the gun. It was at this point that I noticed my shotgun, which I had borrowed off one of the other hunters, did not have a forward sight. I had never used a shotgun before and assumed it was basically the same as a rifle. I'd had plenty of rifle training at school, blasting away with Enfield 303s and Anschutz target rifles at the shooting ranges. But never a shotgun. I was about to point this out to the man who had lent me the gun when I saw that his shotgun was also missing the all-important forward sight, without which I had no idea how anyone would correctly aim the gun. From this, I made the correct assumption that shotguns do not have forward sights. By this time, it was too late to ask for a lesson on how to aim the weapon accurately.

We were hunkered down behind the screen of wood and pine boughs, eyes on the guide, waiting for his signal. Above us and in front, hundreds of geese were coming in to land on the water. Their honking filled the air. The settling mist swirled with the beating of their wings.

When the guide chopped the air with his hand, we threw ourselves at the parapet and began blasting away.

Geese were everywhere. The boom of the shotguns punched at my ears in the confined space of the bunker. Smoke thickened the mist. Sparks from the shotguns sprayed out into the geese, some of which were already floating feet up in the swamp.

My companions were already pausing to reload, but I had not yet fired a shot.

I took aim at a goose, as best I could without the bloody sights, and fired.

I saw one shoot straight up into the air and for a fraction of a second allowed myself some feeling of relief that I had not totally wasted the day.

Almost at the same moment, I heard the guide bellow, "Who shot my decoy?"

All eyes slowly turned to me.

Later, I posed for a photo in between two of the other hunters. They are each holding a goose. I am holding the remains of a decoy.

Time has not erased my shame.

Fishing, too, lost its appeal. Once I began working on deep-sea fishing boats, I came to the sad conclusion that there are only so many times you can stand up to your knees in mackerel, cod, or squid, and still look forward to catching them one at a time.

I can only imagine how badly things might have gone for me if I had been a fourth man in the Colony, ranked even lower than Ivar the cook, in his failing struggle to boil a potato.

But I would rather have one of Ivar's potatoes than go through another baptism of Joika. Bogg and Sodd, at least, bore some passing resemblance to British Army compo rations. But the only thing Joika resembles is another tin of Joika. I should point out that Joika is, I suppose, a genuine taste of hard-core Laplander food. As one of the few truly nomadic people left on Earth, their lives up in the Arctic tundra are filled with hardship. To them, my life would seem absurdly dainty. And so I blame myself that the slightly sour taste of mushy reindeer meatballs in sticky gravy came as a surprise not only to my taste buds but also, soon after, to my digestive system.

It will be of use to future travelers if I note that Joika should, in my opinion, be eaten alone and far from anyone you plan to call a friend in the future.

There are dishes plenty more challenging than Joika. When people talk about gruesome traditional meals in Norway, the word lutefisk inevitably comes up. This is dried fish that has been cured in lye. It is soaked and then boiled into a kind of jelly before being eaten. Lutefisk is, in turn, outranked in the pantheon of nasty Scandinavian victuals by Icelandic specialties of ram's testicles pickled in whey, shark meat that has been buried in the ground until it is putrefied, and squashed sheep's head.

Relatively speaking, Joika isn't so bad. For all I know, a slice of toast decked with Patum Pepperium might be snubbed by the average Laplander.

Pressing on toward Memurubu, I cross the narrow Sigurdtinden ridge, which affords me a view of certain death on either side, before the path slopes down toward the lodge.

Memurubu lodge is clean and new, flanked by a number of old-style tar-beamed huts that occupy the sloping ground that leads down to the water. I read in Andrew Stevenson's *Summer Light* that the old lodge burned down in August 1998. Apparently somebody's socks caught fire. If they had been my socks in their present condition, the combustion would have been spontaneous. While the new lodge is beautiful, I cannot hide my sadness at what I've missed, especially if the tarred huts are any reflection of the way the original structure must have looked.

Retrieving my pack from the dock, I find a little patch of grass down by the water. Here the trees form a perfect windbreak, and, after pitching my tent, I take a swim in the lake. Then I lie on my sleeping bag, watching the comings and goings of the few guests staying at the lodge. As the afternoon turns to evening, I see a few people straggling down out of the mountains. They are walking the trail from Gjendesheim, the same one I plan to walk tomorrow.

Fatigue rushes toward me like a wave. It towers above me, the way the breakers did when I bodysurfed on Narragansett beach. How long ago? But even before I can answer my own thoughts, the wave has tumbled over me, and I am swept away in the black tide of sleep.

I WAKE AT FIVE A.M. to the sound of the rain on my flysheet. Bleary-eyed, I unzip the tent and look out. The world has been reduced to the monochromatic fuzz of an old and out-of-focus photograph. The lake is as gray as new iron, and glinting like the scales of a salmon.

After pulling on my boots, I crawl out of the tent and look toward the Besseggen ridge. But it is not there. The clouds are draped like parachute shrouds over the high ground. The path, which snakes up into the mist, has become a little stream. The rain dappling my face is so cold it feels like minute electric shocks.

I notice a man standing in front of one of the old tar huts. He is wearing only his boots and his underpants. His hands are on his hips, and he stares at the cloud-muffled ridge. Even at a distance, I can see the scowl on his face. He notices me, and we exchange weary glances. Then, simultaneously, we turn away and spit. There will be no climbing today, and I do not have the luxury of time to wait it out inside the confines of my tent.

At first I am annoyed. On the map, there is a symmetry to this hike along Lake Gjende, the lodges spaced evenly apart, promising grand views in all directions. To do only a part of it creates a strange discord in my head.

But then I remember a chapter from *Three in Norway*. It is aptly titled "Misery" and speaks of the same rain that is falling on me now.

"It rained all night again and all day. This was dreadful.... The camp today presented a most cheerless prospect. The canoes were drawn up on land and turned bottom upwards; the kitchen stowed away under a soaked sack; a very third-rate camp fire smoldering before the tent, surrounded by old eggshells, backbones of fish, bacon-rind and some apology for firewood, our two rods standing up against the gloomy sky with the wind whistling through their lines, and all the scenery blotted out with rain and mist, and scudding never-ending clouds that drifted down the valley, and gave very occasional glimpses of extremely wet mountains."

Strangely, the description of this dire scene makes me feel better. Through the pages of their book, the men of the Colony are commiserating with me. It is almost as if they appear out of the grainy air, in their damp wool coats, dripping deerstalker caps, and sodden leather boots, telling me to keep my chin up.

Unlike some of the other writers, whose wandering paths have crossed my own and will again before I leave this country, I am saying good-bye to the men of the Colony. I will miss them. Perhaps, some day far in the future, our fellowship of ghosts will appear on this spot, to ease the mind of other rain-discouraged travelers not yet born.

Chapter Seven
"Words Are Not for Such Things"

BY THE TIME I PASS THROUGH LOM, THE RAIN HAS STOPPED and I am squinting again in the bright sun. I don't know whether to curse the weather gods for chasing me from Lake Gjende or to thank them for letting me continue my journey under the searing blue sky of this early September afternoon.

I have rented a car, no longer willing to be bound by bus timetables, and head into the wilds of the western Jotunheimen mountains. This is the land of Slingsby and Tjernagel, two favorites on my list of long-dead travel companions.

The eastern and western flanks of the Jotunheimen mountains are sandwiched between two roads, 51 and 55, which run roughly north–south and provide any hiker lost in the Jotunheimen with the vague assurance that, if you just keep walking east or west, you will eventually reach civilization. That is, unless you get lost in the winter, in which case you will find the western road, and possibly the eastern road as well, closed by red metal booms, and you would be lucky to get out alive.

Route 51, as I am now discovering, slaloms along the Boverdal valley, tracing the course of the Leira River, whose fast-flowing robin's egg–colored water almost out-greens the pastureland on either side. Here, the fall colors have arrived earlier than at Lake Gjende. The valleys are bronzed with turning leaves. Hay cut from the tilted fields hangs drying on fences made of poles with lengths of wire stretched between them. The haystacks are patroled by magpies and ravens, who strut stiff-legged along the fence tops.

The farmsteads are built in traditional fashion, with huge tarred logs whose stacked ends remind me of the knuckles of hands folded in prayer. Beside these are storehouses, called stabbur, built up on stone foundations and with planked walkways leading up to the thickly turfed roofs. These are for the goats, which are allowed to roam about up there, trimming the tops off dandelions. Through the open door of one storehouse, I see shelves of cheeses, stacks of flatbread, and dried hams hanging from the ceiling. The doors themselves are made from planks linked in upward pointing chevrons with big iron rings for handles and iron studs blistering the woodwork. The top story of the larger storehouses is larger than the ground floor, giving the building a lopsided appearance. I have read that these upper stories house winter clothing and family chests, most of which are painted with the floral motifs known as rosemaligen, designed to remind Norwegians of their flower-filled summers after winter has shellacked their world in ice.

Some of these stabbur have ornately carved panels on the main supports. The snakelike interlocking designs are made more beautiful by time and weather, which has cracked and faded the panels, like those of the stave church back in Lom.

Except for the occasional satellite dish, some of them discreetly camouflage painted, or the red and mud-splashed paint of Massey-Fergusson tractors, the buildings I drive past today are no different from the ones I found in a 1935 issue of NATIONAL GEOGRAPHIC. On this road, you could be forgiven for thinking you had driven back through time. You could also make the bigger mistake of thinking that people held on to buildings like this because they could not afford to upgrade to more modern materials.

Holding on to the traditional is an act of stubbornness, but also of practicality. Local materials are easily replaced using skills that must have been handed down since the days when elder brothers stayed to till the soil and second sons sharpened their war axes and rode off in dragon-prowed ships to seek their fortunes.

Above, on the precarious upland slopes, I see tractors whose front ends are weighted with concrete blocks to stop them from tipping over. Beyond them lie the saeter huts, connected with the main farmstead by cables, which look like chairless ski lifts.

Soon the road begins to climb, and I reach the village of Bovertun, where a few campsites huddle beside the overhanging cliffs. Across the road from a small restaurant is the road to Juvasshytte, where I am to rendezvous with N. Tjernagel, author of the 1917 travel memoir *Walking Trips in Norway*. I stop at the restaurant for a cup of coffee and, except for the woman who pours it, I am the only person there. The empty tables, sunk in gloomy unlit shadows, are neatly set. When I glance up, I see the woman looking at me through the clear plastic of the cake display stand. As our eyes connect, she looks away. When I glance back a moment later, she is watching me again. Once more she looks away. The place is unbearably quiet, the shadows of the hills cold and suffocating.

I wish Tjernagel were here. He would understand. Finding himself in a similarly hemmed-in place, he wrote, "I decided then and there that I should never wish to live in a mountain valley."

Tjernagel is—I cannot bring myself to write "was" since, although he must be long gone by now, he seems so alive to me that for my own sake I must restore him, and his journey, to life—the only man of Norwegian descent whose work I have brought with me, but in many ways he is more removed, and less prepared, for his travels than any of the others.

He came on a pilgrimage, to visit the site of his old family homestead at Follinglo near Fagernes. His grandfather, whose last name was also Follinglo, had emigrated to the United States long ago. What Tjernagel found when he arrived at Follinglo was a draughty old farmhouse, caulked with moss and roofed with birch-bark shingles. Thinking of his grandfather in this sad and run-down place, Tjernagel wrote, "The friends of his youth were no more and I had no cause to linger."

But Tjernagel was mistaken. Soon after, he discovered an ancient woman named Marit, living by herself in a nearby hut. She recalled his grandfather and welcomed him in like a son, serving him "poisonous" coffee in a mug that she first wiped out with her thumb. He then read the Bible to her while she puffed at her pipe and no, I did not get the pronouns wrong in that sentence.

Effectively, the purpose of his visit was at an end. If it had in fact ended there, Tjernagel would not have had much to write home about. But he caught sight of the Jotunheimen's snowy peaks glimmering in the distance, and, like Slingsby, like Clutterbuck, like Simpson, and like me, was drawn hypnotically toward them.

But entirely unlike the others, Tjernagel made no attempt to outfit himself for the journey. In his own words, "I had not the regulation tourist trappings, consisting of heavy boots, thick clothing, rain proof coat and a bag of extra raiment on my back but merely an every day outfit of calfskin shoes, rubbers, light underclothing, cheviot suit and ulster, a standup collar, stiff hat, and a faded-looking umbrella to top off with."

In this "every day outfit," I see a thin and pinch-faced man, pale and with dark hair parted severely down the middle. He is wiry and stubborn and, although a loner like the others, it is more because of temperament than choice. With this, I offer the usual apology, having nothing more to go on than some vague line drawings in the text, and the ghostly face that speaks his words.

More certain is the idea that Tjernagel must go down as one of the most ludicrously under-equipped mountaineers in history. He even makes me feel good about my vintage spork and 1918-dated mess tin.

He tried to cover for this by gloating that his umbrella proved "as a protection from the pelting, driving rain, to which my umbrella-less guide was mercilessly exposed." There is even an illustration of him strolling across a boulder field, looking rather smug as his guide pushes on ahead of him.

A few pages on, we see him in a less dignified position, as he slides down the side of a glacier, watched by several other climbers, none of whom seem to be in trouble. Even the women in this picture, garbed in ankle-length dresses as was the norm for female climbers of the day, are better off than Tjernagel: "I was soon sliding down that awful slope toward a probable abyss at its foot. With my dignity to preserve, and a borrowed camera clutched in my left hand, I manipulated the lifesaving umbrella in my right to such effect that it broke from a stab I made into a cleft in the ice, but which, luckily, arrested my unwilling course, promising safety for a second or two. All my blood seemed to rush into my head and every hair was straining to remove my hat. My mind was a blank and my eyes stared with apprehension. While in this situation, my comrades, almost equally helpless [with laughter?], called to me: 'Take off your rubbers!' This advice I very meekly followed."

Somehow, Tjernagel manages to make it sound as if his umbrella has saved him, when in fact he should be reaching the conclusion that his unwillingness to buy the proper stuff has almost gotten him killed.

The drive to Juvasshytte is equally perilous, on a road so murderously switchbacked that on the map it looks like a varicose vein beneath the wrinkled skin of the mountains. I am stopped twice by toll booths. The first is simply a metal box demanding money, for which envelopes are provided. I do not reach the second until I have twisted and turned past the pines, past the birch, and out at last onto the tundra. This one, located near the Raudbergstulen lodge, has a boom and an electronic ticket machine. Some of the hairpins in this road are so precarious that I feel as if it ought to be dispensing money as a prize for having come this far rather than collecting it.

I pause outside the car, whose engine seems to be gasping for breath as its temperature gauge nudges up into the red.

There is something almost fortlike about the Raudbergstulen lodge. It is the only building for a considerable distance, with a snow fence built around its solid and traditional-built huts. The land here is devoid of anything to halt the wind, which must knife across this plain with merciless cold at other times of year. The swallowtailed Norwegian flag flying from the main lodge building seems to shudder nervously in the faint breeze, as if expecting worse to come. On the other side of Bovertun valley, where I imagine the café lady still sitting motionless behind her cash register, the horizon is scalloped with the mountains of the Bakkebergsfjellet and the Netosaeterfjellet. The colors remind me of the tangled patterns in my old Harris Tweed jacket, hanging on the back of my study chair three thousand miles away. Shadows of cloud slither across the distant slopes, before tumbling like avalanches into the greener fields below.

Ahead, the gravel road snakes up into the treeless hills. There are no barriers to save the lives of careless drivers. If you take the corner too wide, you go off the end of the Earth.

None too soon for my car's engine, the ground levels out upon a plain of crumbled stone. To my left, a vast throne of ice sits at the edge of a glacial lake called the Juvvatnet.

Just past it is the Juvasshytte, a rickety-looking wooden building that is offered no protection from the elements. Tjernagel was right on the mark when he described this as "an eerie spot on the very outskirts of the habitable world." Why the great mountaineer Knut Vole chose such a place to build his lodge, as opposed to anywhere else on this moonscape, seems almost pointless to wonder. The Juvasshytte is like a ship drifting out in the middle of an ocean whose water has vanished, leaving it stranded. Adding to this feeling of a washed-up ship are the iron cables that stretch from the corners of the building. These anchor the building to the ground, from which it would otherwise be blown away.

Adding to this sense of desolation is the fact that the lodge is unexpectedly closed, effectively putting an end to my plan to climb Galdhopiggen mountain. Grumbling, I kick some stones around the parking lot. Galdhopiggen would have been a feather in my cap, since it shares the mantle of Norway's highest mountain with another one named Glittertind. The reason for this sharing of what one would assume is an absolute is that the height of these two peaks is regularly altered by the buildup of snow of their respective summits. The top of Galdhopiggen is flanked by ice from the Styggebrean glacier, which requires, I have been told, a knowledgeable guide to help with the crossing. It is not encouraging that Styggebrean means "dangerous glacier" and there are no guides here today. In Tjernagel's day, Vole himself led people up and down the mountain, for which purpose he built the Juvasshytte in 1884.

This was no small feat considering that there was no road when he began construction and that all the materials had to be carried up from the valley below. Even this achievement pales beside Vole's construction of a second hut on the top of Galdhopiggen itself.

Vole is long gone now, having died in 1929 at the age of eighty. His sharp-nosed, whiskered face is stamped in bronze relief on a plaque, showing him in mid-stride up his beloved mountain. As with all the others I have brought back to life, I had almost convinced myself he would be there waiting for me, as he was when Tjernagel arrived, exhausted from his climb out of the nearby Spiterstulen valley.

Vole was unimpressed by Tjernagel's accomplishment, and unsmilingly told him that another such "reckless excursion" was likely to get him killed. Vole went on to appraise Tjernagel's choice of climbing gear "with a half-scornful, pitying expression in his eyes."

Nevertheless, Vole agreed to serve as guide for Tjernagel, who must be the only man in history ever to have summited this mountain wearing calfskin city shoes.

At the peak of Galdhopiggen, Tjernagel experienced a kind of awakening. Having tacked his calling card to the wall of the summit hut, where thousands who came before him had also left their names, he struggled to find words to describe that particular combination of physical exhaustion and a view beyond the imagination of all who have not seen it for themselves. "Here," he wrote, "was a glimpse of heaven, a foretaste of the beyond."

Sitting in the car, which shudders now and then from gusts of wind, I read these words again. I shudder inside, too, at this haunting repetition of my own first glimpse of the Rondane. What is it about this place? I ask myself. Why do I feel as if I am entering another realm, which seems to straddle the real and the imaginary, and in doing so breaks down not only the boundaries of space but also of time? I sense the presence of my dead companions as much as if they sat beside me now, peering over my shoulder.

I know how crazy it sounds to write of "presences," but in light of my own experience, as well as of Tjernagel and the others, not mentioning them seems even crazier.

And even if one were to discount those men and me as well, the surly but good-natured Knut Vole, a practical man if ever one lived, was not without his own blunt revelation. In trying to find words to describe not only the extraordinary labors of his life, but the ultimate reason for those labors, Vole could only utter that "words are not for such things."

Tjernagel himself continued to grapple with his thoughts, trying to convey what it was that had changed him: "The messages received here are private, untranslatable and not deliverable through carriers or interpreters.... There comes over me a sense of the vast solitude encompassing me."

I get out of the car. At that same moment, a hollow boom sounds from the dirt-crusted Kjelen glacier that feeds Juvvatnet Lake. The ice is cracking, somewhere deep beneath its frozen skin. Tjernagel heard this, too. "All was silence," he reported, "save the warring winds and booming glacier."

I look up to the crest of Galdhopiggen and can just make out the hut on the top, where the bare rock is bearded by slicks of blue ice.

I could chance it, I think. I should chance it. I must not be afraid. Tjernagel was afraid, and he said he would climb Galdhoppigen not in spite of his fear but because of it.

Then I catch sight of a warning posted on a sign beside the memorial to Vole. It spells out, with ghastly simplicity, exactly why I am not going to attempt to climb Galdhopiggen on my own.

According to this sign, the glacier moves at a rate of thirty meters a year, creating crevasses that are sometimes fifty meters deep. Over these crevasses thin layers of snow and ice form, creating what are called "ice bridges." If you fall through one of these ice bridges and are not secured by a rope to another climber, you will fall fifteen to twenty meters until your head gets stuck between the ice walls. "Some survive such falls," the sign informs me, "but not for very long, for ice cold water runs down the walls and you will freeze to death quickly without help."

There is no way around it. I wander out across a quiltlike field of mossy rocks until I reach a nameless slope that shears away into the valley of the Visa River. Except for an old and empty smoke grenade canister, which speaks of some long-ago cry for help, I find no sign that man has ever set foot in this place.

As I drive back down the mountain, I can't help wondering if Vole ever regretted all his efforts to make Galdhopiggen more accessible. Surely he must have looked on poorly equipped people like Tjernagel as a liability, not only to themselves but to the reputation of the mountain. It doesn't take much to choke the spirit out of a place, and in trying to share what was magical about it, I wonder if Vole might have seen that magic trampled down into the snow by the thousands of people he led across its slopes.

One glance in my rearview mirror reassures me. Galdhopiggen towers in the distance, its summit blazing white against the cloudless sky. Whatever spell these mountains conjure on the minds of those who see them, defying us to frame within the boundary of words the sum of all their overwhelming beauty, will never fade away.

Chapter Eight

Elementals

LEAVING BOVERTUN, THE ROAD CLIMBS UP THE NARROW Breidsoeterdalen valley toward the lodge known as Krossbu. The small cluster of red buildings occupy, as Tjernagel phrased it, "a bleak site not far from the rim of a mighty drift." This "drift" is actually Leirbrean glacier, whose turquoise ice glimmers in the evening light.

I see no cars in the parking lot, and wonder if this place is closed, too. It is late in the season, nearing the time of year when these lodges shut down for the winter. With the first snows, the roads too will be closed, leaving the Jotunheimen to sleep under its mantle of ice.

Hesitantly I climb the worn steps and tug at the door. To my relief, it opens. A little bell jingles on the door handle. The warm, damp smell of boiling potatoes and poaching salmon floods into my lungs.

Inside, the walls are patched with photographs of trips across the Leibrean glacier. Well-worn but comfortable-looking furniture fills a sitting room off to one side. It is all mismatched, as are the lamp shades. The ceilings are low and the floors uneven. All this only adds to the cozy feeling of the place, contrasting sharply with the bareness of Krossbu's location and the weather-beaten paint on its exterior.

A tall, thin woman with dark hair hands me a key and informs me that dinner is in one hour. A certain finality in her voice leaves me in no doubt that I had better be on time if I want to get anything to eat.

I ask if I am the only guest.

"No," she says, and that is all.

Feeling somewhat rebuffed by the lack of conversation, I head upstairs to my room. The place is bigger than it looks from the outside. My room is tiny, with two sleigh-type beds. In the corner is an old iron stove, on which a card gives strict instructions that it is not to be used.

Except for the whine of an occasional car on its way up to the wilderness of the Sognefjellet plateau, the place is so quiet that the air seems almost to hiss, as if I can hear the actual movement of Earth hurtling through space.

It was a very different scene when Tjernagel passed through here. Having walked the length of the Breidsoeterdalen valley, he arrived to find the Krossbu lodge so crowded that the only place for him to sleep was on the floor. This is not as unusual as it might seem. In these mountains, no traveler is turned away from a lodge. To do so, particularly in Tjernagel's day, might condemn a person to death out on the tundra.

The wind from Juvasshytte still burns against my face. When I close my eyes, my brain seems to thump from one side of my head to the other, and I see again the mad twists and turns of the road. I want to lie down and go to sleep, but I know that if I do, even my alarm clock will not wake me and I will sleep through dinner.

On my arrival at Krossbu, I noticed a sign that hiking boots are not to be worn inside the building. I should have brought some slippers, but all I have are socks. My last clean pair, I discover, have holes in the heels. I suppose I ought not to care, but the combination of my sun-reddened cheeks and travel-worn clothes makes me ashamed of my disheveled state. Borrowing a trick from George Orwell's Down and Out in Paris and London, I take my pen and ink in the places where my skin shows through the holes in the dark blue wool of the socks. Then I run the tap, bathe my face in icy water, put on my least dirty shirt, and, with the dignity of a tramp, head back downstairs.

The dining room, about ten paces long by about four paces wide, is painted with soft shades of green and blue. The long tables are all empty except for one, at which two old men are sitting. They speak in hushed voices, as if the silence of the room commands it. As I walk in, they glance up, nod, and return to their talk.

I find myself a spot at another table and crack open my old leather-bound notebook, ready to transcribe the jumble of details of my day. My pen has run out, and I am reduced to scribbling with the toothpick-size ballpoint that is part of my Swiss Army knife.

As I write, a young man emerges from the kitchen, wiping his hands on his apron. His knuckles are red from washing dishes. With the same severity I noticed in the woman who handed me my key, he advances toward my table. "You are having dinner?" he asks.

"Yes, please."

Without another word, he gestures toward the two old men, indicating that I am to sit with them.

I seem to have broken an unspoken rule of the place, but some rules you never learn until you break them. Feeling as if I have committed some unforgivable faux pas, I sheepishly make my way to the other table and sit down, already wishing I had forgone the meal and passed out in my room instead.

As the boiled salmon and potatoes are put in front of me, I prepare to gulp my dinner and be gone. But the two men seem to know that I meant them no offense. In fact, quite the opposite. I only meant not to intrude.

They introduce themselves, in perfect English, as schoolteachers from Helsingborg in southern Sweden. The elder of the two is a professor, Gunnar Carlsson. He has a kind face and ruddy cheeks. The other man, Anders Hellborg, is wiry and thoughtful, leaving Professor Carlsson to do the talking.

Each autumn for more than twenty-seven years, they have led trips of Swedish high school students into the hills around Krossbu, whose landscape contrasts as starkly with that of Helsingborg as it does with the flatlands of central New Jersey. If I have come here for peace and quiet, they tell me, I had better enjoy it while I can, because later this evening an entire busload of high school kids are arriving for a week of mountain climbing.

While I can imagine the thought of so many high school kids striking fear and loathing into the hearts of tranquility-loving travelers, I remain unfazed. After fifteen years of teaching at a boarding school, the last thing that will rattle me is the chaos about to descend on this place.

Once I explain the reason for my lack of panic, the three of us settle back into the instant familiarity, which transcends all boundaries of age and language, shared by those who are engaged in the same profession.

Professor Carlsson has retired from teaching, but still likes to lead these tours. Both he and Hellborg have each spent more than a year of their lives at the Krossbu lodge. Carlsson's specialty is science, and he informs me that he has spent many years studying the scourge of the black fly, not only here in Scandinavia but all over the world. I know these rotten little creatures from my summers up in Maine. They are a bad business, crawling behind your ears, under your watch strap, or down the collar of your shirt and leaving you a few moments later with bloody welts that take a week to go away. I usually have to deal with them only for a week or two when I am there, since I arrive just as their season is ending. By the Fourth of July, they are mostly gone, and the aggravation caused by mosquitoes, who rule the still air and the darkness for the remainder of the summer, seems like nothing in comparison.

But it is clear from the way he speaks that Professor Carlsson has a softness in his heart for them; the efficiency of their species, their rude effectiveness, and their tenacity. There are places in northern Sweden, he tells me, where I could be sitting across a table from him, the way I am now, and there would be so many black flies in the air that I would have trouble seeing him. At first I think he must be joking, but then from the expression on his face, I realize he is serious and shudder at the thought of such a swarm.

Hellborg listens with one ear to these stories, which he must have heard many times before. His thoughts appear elsewhere, and he sits with his hands folded in his lap, dividing the last of the Bull's Blood wine they have been sharing between their two glasses. The little black plastic bull dangles from its leash at the neck of the bottle. Across the room, on a wooden cup rack, literally hundreds of these black plastic bulls are arranged, as if taking part in a miniature stampede.

After the meal, we wander into the empty sitting room and stretch out on the couches. Tjernagel found the place so packed that he had to stand in the corner, "hugging the almost useless stove." On seeing a woman fling open the window, allowing "icy air to sweep down from the adjacent glacier directly into our very laps and lungs," he imparted his "well-formulated ideas regarding such contrary females" to the man standing next to him, only to learn, too late, that the man was her husband. Tjernagel, reduced almost to tears of embarrassment, confides that "It is always rather unsafe to discuss one's neighbors thus."

For a while Carlsson and Hellborg and I pore over books of wild-flowers, which I attempt unsuccessfully to match against a list I made before I left the States.

In the kitchen, a television is broadcasting a soccer game. The jabber of the commentator is punctuated with groans and sighs from the cook, whose team appears to be losing.

I realize that the grandfather clock on the other side of the room has just stopped ticking. Then I understand that the ticking sound is in fact the methodical rattle of the hot water pipes. The clock has probably been out of order since Tjernagel's day. Even its hands are missing. There could be no better way to sum up the lodge at Krossbu.

In the glowing violet dusk, I stare through windowpanes fogged with condensation. Away to the east, a row of vicious peaks line the horizon. The most daunting of these is Smorstabbtinden, which, along with its neighbor Storbreatinden, cuts the sky like shards of broken glass set into the top of a wall to discourage trespassers. The purpose of these mountains seems no different. The Jotunheimen are, after all, not the province of man but of the Jotun, frost giants who are enemies of men and gods alike. The Jotun claimed this land long before man and even before the gods to whom men used to pray. They are part stone, part ice, part flesh, patching their bodies with the flayed skins of those who are foolish enough to wander into their land. They are shape-shifters, morphing into wolves or eagles. The name Jotun means "one who devours," and in their wild and vicious presence is personified all the turbulence of nature in this northern world.

Darkness crowds against the windows.

Somewhere, out there in the night, the busload of Swedish students are approaching. Carlsson and Hellborg enjoy their last few moments of peace.

I feel as if I ought to leave them to it, but there is still one thing I want to know. "Why this place?" I ask.

Carlsson and Hellborg both smile. They make vague gestures with their hands, and noncommittal sounds escape their lips. My impression is not that they don't know. They do know. Of course they know. They have been coming here for twenty-five years. It is more a question of putting it into words.

"There is a vibration here," says Hellborg.

"A vibration?" I ask.

He sighs. "Perhaps that is not the right word."

I sit back and fold my arms. "Vibration," I say quietly.

Carlsson is watching me with glacier blue eyes.

We sit for a long moment in silence.

"But you understand what I mean," he says at last.

It almost catches me by surprise that I do in fact know what he means. Despite the severity of the landscape here, harsh even in a world of harshness, there is some strange but undeniable feeling of balance, as if somehow the builders of the Krossbu lodge had stumbled upon the axis of the world.

Carlsson is still hunting for the right words. He decides to explain it in perhaps the only way it can be explained, with a story.

"There's a valley north of here," he says. "It is called Brangsdalen."

At the mention of the word, I see Hellborg stiffen. Something in what Carlsson is about to tell me has woken him from his half-paid attention.

"Each year, we take the students there," continues Carlsson. "There is no path. You must follow the map. On the way, you can see pits that are dug in the ground for catching reindeer. These pits are a thousand years old."

"It is pretty in the Brangsdalen valley," says Hellborg, as if to lead his old friend back into the telling of his story.

"And twice," says Carlsson, "in the years we have been going there, students have seen things."

"Things?" I ask. "What things?"

Carlsson narrows his eyes a little, as if unsure whether to continue. "Ghosts?" I ask.

He shakes his head, but I see from his expression that at least we are on the same page. "The first time, a young woman saw some kind of human shape, but it was made up of light. Green-brown light. This young woman was gifted. She could tell when people were suffering. She knew when people were going to die. When she saw this thing, she was very upset and she asked that I not tell any of the other students. Then, a few years later, a young man also saw this thing."

"But what was it?" I ask.

"There is a name for them. These things have been sighted all over the world, and the description of them is so similar that they have received a classification. They are called 'Elementals.'"

At first, I just shake my head, sure I have never heard that word before. But then, rising from the well of half-forgotten thoughts comes the realization that I have indeed heard that word before. And now the hair stands up on my arms, because I first learned of Elementals from an Englishman named Algernon Blackwood, in his account of a journey he once made into the outer reaches of the Danube. He titled his story "The Willows." It is the most frightening thing I have ever read.

Here, in this hut at the end of the world, the whole story comes tumbling from the closet of my mind.

Around the year 1900, Blackwood and his companion, ironically a Swede, traveled by canoe along the Danube, passing through Vienna and crossing the border into Hungary, somewhere near Pressburg. They found themselves in a place the Hungarians called the Zumpf. Here, the Danube breaks into a hundred different streams, around which grows a wilderness of scrub willow trees. They were warned by the locals not to go there, partly because the irregular rise and fall of the waters might leave them stranded forty miles from anywhere, and partly because the Hungarians believe the willowlands to be a haunted place, some kind of gateway to another world, where the presence of man is not tolerated.

Blackwood dismissed these warnings, as did the imperturbable Swede, and they soon found themselves far from the nearest town, camped upon a little beach beside one of the many rivers that sluiced through the wilderness.

Blackwood was no stranger to camping in remote places, and had developed a sense for whether a campsite was a "welcoming" place or not. There is no doubt about the truth in this. You either feel at ease in a place or you do not, and the reasons for your comfort or discomfort are not always readily explicable. Here, on their first night in the Zumpf, Blackwood began to understand what the locals had been talking about. He did not feel welcome here, and his uneasiness was worsened by the ceaseless blowing of the wind through the willows. The longer this went on, the more Blackwood became convinced that the source of his disquietude was not the wind, but the willows themselves, although he could not understand how this could be so.

Before they turned in for the night, Blackwood and the Swede watched a man drift by them on the river. He was shouting to them as he passed, but they could not hear what he was saying. The man repeatedly crossed himself before disappearing out of sight around the river bend.

They woke the next morning to find that their canoe had been vandalized, and the blade of one canoe paddle bizarrely ground down into uselessness. They spent the day making repairs, keeping their thoughts to themselves as to who or what could have caused such damage. Each man was determined to maintain his hold on the rational world.

But the second night put paid to that.

Blackwood woke in the middle of the night and saw, inches from his face, fingerlike impressions being made into the canvas of the tent. He became convinced that a tree had partially fallen and now hung suspended over the tent and might at any moment topple down on top of them. When he scrambled out into the dark, he saw there was no overhanging tree.

All around him, the willows twisted in the wind. They seemed to have come closer in the dark. Then he noticed things moving in among the willows. He tried to convince himself that it was some trick of light and that these things were the willows themselves, but the shapes had begun to move in the opposite direction to the way the wind was blowing. They were huge, bronze-colored beings, vaguely human in their shape, but in all other aspects quite inhuman. Their bodies melted together and corkscrewed into the air in one huge shifting, living mass.

Neither Blackwood nor the Swede could continue the pretense of nonchalant and rational thought. The standards of reality had changed. The wind itself was walking.

The Swede became convinced that neither of them would ever get out of there alive. He confessed to Blackwood that he had seen the boat and boatman rise from the water, drift past their camp, and sink beneath the water once again. He believed that these beings both had seen among the writhing willow branches, these Elementals, were searching for them at the borders of their own universe but could not find them. They were drawn, the Swede believed, not by sight or smell of touch but by the panic of the men, like a shark toward a bleeding fish.

In the end, they discover a drowned man, whose corpse has been horribly mutilated, washed up on their little beach. The Swede is convinced that he has been butchered by these Elementals, thus sparing the lives of the two travelers.

These images wash over me and then are gone, leaving me once again in the stillness of the Krossbu lodge. No time has passed, although I feel as if it has.

"Elementals," I say.

The two men nod. Neither can lay claim to having seen one, but it is clear that both men believe something was seen. Why these two students should have been singled out, what powers they possessed to give them sight, while the rest remained blind, remains as much of a mystery as the Elementals themselves.

Mystery or not, I know that when the sun comes up tomorrow I must go there, to the valley of Brangsdalen. I am suddenly conscious of everything converging on this place, like beams of sunlight streaming back toward their source. The whole purpose of my journey has not so much changed as expanded. It is as if, without ever knowing it, I have been waiting all my life for some rendezvous with whatever tomorrow will bring me.

The quiet of the evening is broken by the arrival of the bus. Students pour out, glad to stretch their legs after the twelve-hour ride from Sweden.

Carlsson and Hellborg are swept up in their duties, shepherding the students to their respective rooms.

Before turning in for the night, I stand outside on the porch. The darkness hides everything but the sound of running water and the quiet thunder of wind blowing down of the glacier. A line from Blackwood's story keeps repeating in my head: "The Elementals are the true immortals," he wrote. "The gods are here if they are anywhere at all."

NOW I MUST TRY TO DESCRIBE something that I have never written about before. I have never done so because, by not writing about it, I could convince at least a part of myself that it never took place. But it did.

The first novel I wrote was set during the Second World War and told the story of a young German soldier sent to fight against the Americans in December 1944, in what became known as the Battle of the Bulge. The book was based on the experiences of an elderly man I met when I was an exchange student in Germany. His description of the events that changed his life were accurate enough that I was able to pinpoint exactly where he had fought.

He had, as a grenadier in the 12th SS Panzer Division, been involved in a vicious fight for a small town called Rocherath, which lies in the Ardennes forest on the German/Belgian border. In order to be able to write the book, I traveled to Rocherath and walked through the woods where the battle had been fought. I had brought along a tent, in order to camp in the woods.

The Ardennes forest must rank as one of the most mysterious places on Earth. The pine trees grow so thickly that to move through them requires you to flail your arms like a person learning to swim. The branches cut out all but the gloomiest light. On the pine-needled ground, nothing grows except the occasional slimy mushroom. The forest smells damp and rotten. The hunter's trails that snake between the trees are narrow and muddy and seem to lead nowhere.

I had not gone far into the woods before I came across the first signs that soldiers had been here. Foxholes, dug by soldiers of the U.S. 2nd and 99th Divisions, pocked the ground. Some had branches still laid across the top, to protect against the shrapnel of artillery fire. Here and there the gouges of explosions showed in the flinty earth. In these foxholes, I found pieces of old American mess tins, shreds of woolen Army blankets, even the foil packets of Nescafé and powdered lemonade from American C ration packs. Around the rims of these foxholes were hundreds of spent cartridges, attesting to the ferocity of the fighting that had taken place here.

I was stunned to find these things still here. I guess I had expected it all to have been cleared away, the holes filled in, some attempt made to bandage these scars in the dirt. The fact that the pine trees grew so close together had prevented the otherwise normal rate of decay, leaving such fragile mementos as these foil packets still intact. I remember picking up one of the packets and being able to close my fist around it in the exact shape that the soldier had crushed it with his own fist, twenty years before I was born.

The farther I went into the forest, the more junk of war I found. The windshield of a jeep. An unexploded rifle grenade. A pair of boots.

When it grew dark, I pitched my tent and ate a cold meal of bread and the local smoke-cured ham called *jambon d'ardennes.*

I had a thin sleeping bag, which I thought would be sufficient, but with nothing between me and the ground except the floor of the tent and the flimsy stuffing of my sleeping bag, I was freezing.

Eventually, I managed to fall asleep.

The next thing I remember, I was sitting bolt upright, sleeping bag drawn tight around me, listening to something moving just outside the tent.

What happened next makes no sense. Or it doesn't make sense in any way that I can make sense of it. I realized that there was not one but several things moving around outside the tent. I also realized that they were not making any sound. So I could not hear them. Neither could I see them, because the flaps of the tent had been zipped shut. But I was as certain they were out there as if they had been calling to me. And then I realized that they were calling to me. But not with words. I could hear them, but they were not talking.

I was so frightened that I can recall the exact sensations of cold and the sound of the wind blowing in the tops of the trees and the taste of blood in my mouth from having bitten the inside of my cheek.

For a long time, I just sat there, conscious of these things moving around outside the tent and calling to me to come out.

Then they stopped calling and I knew I was alone again.

Sometimes I wonder what would have happened if I had gone out there into the dark. Sometimes I wish I had gone. I wonder if I should have been so afraid. I had gone to those woods to find something, and I think I found it, or it found me, but I was too afraid to look it in the eye.

I pity those students who saw the strange shapes drifting among their friends in the valley at Brangsdal. But I know they are also to be envied. They were forced, as I was, to rethink the once inviolable boundaries of their world. Only then do you get to walk through the looking glass.

Lying down to sleep in the too-short bed, my heels balance on the wooden end frame. It reminds me of my bunk on the fishing boat, which was also too short for my six-foot-two-inch frame. Remembering the boat makes me think of Arneson. I wonder if he is still out there on the water, riding the waves and dreaming of the place he left behind.

I expect to be visited by nightmares, like Scrooge and his Christmas ghosts. But instead I sleep soundly, waking to the murmur of voices down below in the breakfast room, and the creak of floorboards out in the hall as students shuffle back and forth from the showers.

Certainly, I slept better than Tjernagel. By this stage of his journey, he was fast becoming as worn out as his calfskin shoes. A distinctly whiney tone entered his writing, and he "began to wonder at myself for having willingly left a decent bed back home only to bring up in a trap like this."

I have had my share of those nights. Back in my penniless student days, I once spent a night in a left luggage locker at the Gare du Nord in Paris.

But this was not one of those nights. Now sunlight fills the room. Looking out, the sky is so clear and darkly blue that it resembles a vast, upturned bowl carved out of lapis lazuli. These are the days hikers pray for.

After Tjernagel's sleepless night on the floor, he was met with similarly beautiful weather: "There opened up between the peaks, such vistas of glory as made us catch our breath and return thanks to Him who had spread such a feast before us."

After a hurried bowl of porridge, I secure a map from the caretaker, locate Brangsdalen valley, and strap on my pack. I want to tell Carlsson and Hellborg where I am going, in case they might have some last-minute advice, and also to let them know that I have not simply dismissed their stories as it would have been easier to do.

But Carlsson and Hellborg are giving out instructions to the students, who are in the process of assembling their *nistepakker* lunches. These consist of open-faced sandwiches separated by layers of wax paper. The sandwiches are fitted into little metal boxes and stored, along with small thermoses of coffee, for the day ahead.

I cram a sandwich into my pack, wishing I had one of those little boxes and a thermos, too, as I head out into the dazzle of the morning sun.

Crossing the fast-running Bovre River by means of a log bridge, I climb the boggy ground of the Veslfjellet. The only trails are those made by the many sheep, which now and then look up from their grazing and scan me with a haughty look. Sunlight makes halos around the fluffy outlines of their bodies.

Soon I have reached the high ground that runs between a precipice of cliffs and the treeless Veslfjelltinden mountain range. I find myself on a broad plateau called the Storflye. The ground is scattered with boulders, like a huge game of marbles abandoned by the frost giants.

The drop from the cliffs is so sheer that I do not go near the edge. Somewhere down below is the Breidsoeterdalen valley and the road I drove to reach Krossbu. I am, more or less, heading back the way I came, but the separation from the valley below and the plateau I have up here is so complete that it seems to belong to a different world.

Whether it is the sunlight or the openness of the space, I have no fear of being alone up here. I walk a razor edge of shadow cast down by the mountains above. When I step from the sun into the gloom, the drop in temperature strips the warmth from my body like layers peeled off an onion.

I find a reindeer trap on a ledge of rock, with a fall of maybe ten feet down onto another bed of stones. Leading up to the ledge are two lines of rocks, called guiding stones, placed there to steer the frightened reindeer over the edge. The reindeer would break their legs in the fall, and would be quickly dispatched by men waiting out of sight at the base of the ledge.

There is no other trace of human hand upon this ground, to tell me I have not stumbled through some gate of time to find myself a thousand years distant from the world I woke up in this morning.

The sense of solitude is overwhelming, as is my insignificance in this place. I am conscious of the comfort one can take in the simple piles of cairn stones one finds beside the marked trails in these mountains. They are not merely signposts. They are reminders that you are not alone. That people have been here before you. That you are still fixed upon the wheel of human affairs.

But I do not see that now. I do not see these hills, these rivers of ice, these flecks of lichen as Tjernagel's "feast laid out by Him." Instead, I see these mountains as standing in obedience to nothing, in defiance of nothing, without reference to gods or men. What arrogance it seems to believe that all of this was created for the benefit of man. I am conscious of a vast illusion torn away before my eyes, like the canvas of a ruined painting. I have no dominion over this place. Such an idea is more acceptable in a landscape where man-made monuments to ourselves spike the skyline. Here, it becomes like the whimpering of a lost child, afraid to be alone, afraid to die, afraid above all else to be finished and forgotten. Up on this plateau, faced with the once terrible, unthinkable idea that I am not sheltered by the wings of angels, not promised some continuance of life beyond the boundaries of my flesh and blood, I experience a kind of glad annihilation.

Walking on across the plain, I soon come in sight of the Brangsdalen valley. It lies some five hundred feet below me, narrow and green, with a lake at its center. Surrounding the lake is the paler green of marshy ground. There seems to be no clear path down. Cautiously, I begin to make my way down a series of gullies, the stones slick with runoff water. In the mud, I see fresh reindeer tracks as big as my outstretched hand, but no sign of the animals themselves.

Scrambling down from boulder to boulder, I come across the bones of a sheep, laid out on the flat surface of a rock. The bones are patched with green mildew, the vertebrae scattered like dice.

Only when I arrive at the valley floor do I feel in my chest the first flutter of worry. I want to see something, but I am also afraid of seeing it. Echoing in my head is a line from Rilke's Duino Elegies: "Every angel is terrifying."

Professor Carlsson had told me that the place where the students had seen these Elementals was on a spit of land that juts out into the lake. I can see it quite clearly from here, and slowly I begin to make my way toward it. There are some well-worn sheep trails weaving drunkenly from one end of the valley to the other, but no trees or bushes. Nothing taller than grass is growing here. Small streams trickle down the gentler slope on the other side of the valley. Except for the sound of the water, the quiet is complete. Not even the wind, which sings an endless moaning anthem up above.

I reach the edge of the lake. It looks shallow and still, perfectly reflecting the sky.

I wait.

The silence is all around me. It is more than silence. There is a stillness here, which is not the same thing as silence. This stillness is the mark of Sacred Ground. For all of us, there is sacred ground somewhere. It might not be a place of great beauty, or of quiet. But even without these things, there is an almost gyroscopic sense of balance in these locations. There is a place like this in Narragansett, Rhode Island. It is at the end of the beach, where a river called the Narrow River empties out into the sea. On that spit of sand, I have often stood and felt the stillness, even above the rushing of the water and the breeze through the spartina grass. I have given up wondering why this is so. I just know that it is.

Slowly, I lower my pack to the ground, take out my lunch box, and eat my lunch. All the while I keep glancing around. I pump some water out of the lake. Even filtered through my portable purifier, it tastes musty.

When I have finished my lunch, I pack up my stuff and head back toward the place where I came in. I keep turning around and looking back at the lake. I don't know whether to be relieved or disappointed. Climbing out of the valley, I look back a few more times, but then I quit.

Returning to Krossbu, I follow the line of the cliffs past Oy Nufstje Lake, where fish are rising through the Coke-bottle-green water, making bull's-eyes as they touch the surface.

At the shallow end of the lake, I strip down and take a swim. The cold is so shocking that after I have climbed out, the air feels tropical. For a minute, I sit crouched on a rock, sun on my bare back, stirring my fingers in the water.

The first thing I see when I look up makes me gasp. It is the skull of a reindeer, lying on a patch of marshy ground. Antlers still jut from its head. It looks like a creature from some land beneath the ground, come up to see who is walking on the roof of his world. I half expect the eyeless sockets to blink, and for the skull to sink back down below the reeds. But there it stays, bones bleaching in the wind.

Such an idea would have made sense to the ancient Norse and Celts, for whom the world was not shaped in the way we see it now. We are so bound by our belief in the scientific explainability of things that it is hard for us to go back to seeing things as our ancestors did. Here in the north, they lived in a universe of veils, which separated the various worlds of which they were aware. The veils were thinner in some places than in others. Certain rock formations, springs, and trees all served as boundary markers for the worlds. In these "thin" places, you could see across to those other worlds, or even voyage into them if you knew how. Here, it seems to me, that veil is wafer thin, and I am made aware of how much I cannot see, but which I sense is here.

I think there are forms of energy that we cannot yet identify, in the same way that lightning was, for so many thousands of years, a mystery, explainable only in mythic stories. One day, perhaps, this prickling of our senses will at last make sense and find its place among the now-solved mysteries of our species.

That evening, the Krossbu dining room is crowded with students, so I head up to my room and dine on crispbread and Turistproviant, washed down with the water from the nameless lake in Brangsdalen valley. It is meager fare, but I am as content in this bare-walled place as I would be at the best table in Le Cirque.

Later that evening, after hanging my damp clothes in the drying room, I make my way downstairs. Tired students lounge in chairs, on couches, on the floors.

Professor Carlsson is there, the only one still on his feet. His cheeks are ruddy with fresh air. "Did you go?" he asks.

"I was there," I tell him. "It is a peaceful place."

He nods, and knows my meaning. Like him, I saw no Elementals there, but he knows as well that I did not return here empty-handed. The stillness of the Brangsdalen valley has found its way inside me, like the water I drank from its lake.

We smile and say good night. There is nothing more to say. Knut Vole was right. Words are not for such things.

Chapter Nine

I See Myself Dead

AFTER BREAKFAST THE NEXT MORNING, I SET OFF FOR Smorrstabbtinden.

Over coffee one hour before, Carlsson told me how he and eighteen of his students climbed that broken bottle of a mountain on the horizon. As he spoke, I looked from Carlsson to the horizon and back to Carlsson, amazed that a man in his sixties should be able not only to scale such a beast of rock but should do so at the head of a group of inexperienced climbers. This lulled me into a feeling of confidence in my own abilities, a feeling I am soon to regret.

Clouds have gathered in the valley. Following a muddy path beside the tumbling Leira River, I quickly settle into the rhythm of my marching. The weight of my pack, and the unevenness of the trail, keeps my head bowed toward the ground. My route passes through areas of swampy ground where spongy black soil oozes even blacker water where my feet press down upon it. Shaggy tufts of cotton grass cluster on patches of electric green moss.

I pass through the veil of mist into the sunlit uplands of the Veslf-jellet. The angles of Smorrstabbtinden seem to change each time I raise my head to look at it. The mountain is formed like a staircase with six enormous steps. One side consists of a sheer cliff face, which borders the expanse of the Leirbrean glacier. As usual, I have no visual marker by which to judge its scale, so I do not know whether it will take me a few hours or the rest of the day to reach its summit.

Ahead, the reedy grass gives way to the crumbled stone of terminal moraine, ground up and spat out by the endlessly gnawing teeth of the glacier. Dozens of small cairns dot the way. They look like people praying on their knees.

My father, who was a geophysicist specializing in paleomagnetics, spent a lot of time in places like this. He died so young, at the age of forty-three, and spent so much time away, that I never really got to know him. Twenty-six years later, what I recall is mostly from pictures, many of which show him on the moraine slopes of Iceland's Vattnajokull glacier, where he drilled for rock samples, which he would later use for carbon dating.

My father was six foot six, with a craggy Roman nose and crooked front teeth, a size eight head and size thirteen feet. He was a stubborn and outspoken man. People either loved him or despised him, and I do not think he cared either way. He belonged out here, I think, away from the gentleness of things. And if ghosts do exist, he is out there still, in his scuffed boots and stained clothes, chipping away with a rock hammer at the shinbones of the world.

From among the stones, two gray birds break cover. I recognize them as upland ptarmigan, or fjallrype. They are cousins of the low-land fjallrype, but with coloring more suited to a life among the silt and stones. Their plumage is gray with flecks of black and white, and their legs are thick with cream-colored feathers, making them look as if they are wearing little sheepskin boots. The male has a dull orange crescent above his eye, like a bald eyebrow. He straggles off, feigning injuries and leading me away from their nest, just like the other fjall-rype I have seen.

I pause beside the pearl-hazy water of Leirvatnet Lake, which hugs the edge of the glacier. From a point six feet above the level of the lake, a stream of water pours out of the ice, like bilge being pumped out of an ocean liner. The shore of the lake is thick gray mud, pow-der fine where it has dried against the rocks.

Above, chalking the otherwise unblemished sky, is the contrail of a jet. The jet itself looks like a chip of ice, as if a fragment of the glacier has been sent hurtling through space. It seems so out of place that for a moment I am as baffled by its presence as the people would have been who built the reindeer traps a thousand years before. I think about the people up there, belted into their uncomfortable seats, struggling to open their packets of peanuts and nervously waiting for turbulence to shake them like a toy in the hands of an angry child.

Back on Earth, the trail seems to have vanished. A basin of rock and ice stand between me and the mountain.

I begin to skirt the edge of the glacier, slowly gaining ground toward the first of the giant steps that make up Smorrstabbtinden. The bones of lemmings, scraps of wet fur still clinging to them, lie scattered on the ice. I wonder if they were brought there by some hunting bird or if they lost their way and froze to death out here.

Climbing an almost vertical wall of earth and rock, I finally reach level ground. From here I pick up the faint trace of a path, which winds up the side of the mountain.

Out across the distant ice, I spot a line of people roped together, looking like Morse code dashes and dots as they march across the glacier.

Now the climbing grows hard. There is almost no soil. Most of the mountain is simply rock, some of it in such fantastic shapes that I find myself hallucinating the forms of living creatures. Some are serrated, like the teeth of half-invented beasts set aside by their creator and extinct before they ever came to be. Others are precisely split into overlapping plates like the skin of armadillos. There are pink rocks, green rocks, black rocks spliced with white like fossilized Irish coffees. Each stone promises to tilt and crush my ankle against its neighbor like a trap, but these traps were set too long ago and their jaws have rusted shut.

Somewhere on the third step, I reach a point where I can go no farther. It is not until I look back that I realize how steep the angle has become. I scrabble to the left and then over to the right, hoping for some lead to open up. However Carlsson and his students climbed this mountain, it was not by this route.

For the first time in my life, I am paralyzed by vertigo. I cling to the rock face, sweating. But I can't stand the thought of giving up. I refuse to surrender to this mountain. I am gripped by a kind of madness. It is as if the survival of my body depends on going back down, but the survival of my mind depends on continuing. I hoist myself up and immediately lose my grip on the slippery rocks. With a shout, I slide back, sending a stream of grit rattling down among the boulders I have climbed to get this far. My hands catch, then my feet, and I am safe again. Above me, the crest of the mountain snubs the powdery sky. I have never seen such darkly burning blue.

Cursing with frustration, I reach the less suicidal angles of the lower steps. At the edge of the Storbrean glacier, which nudges up against the other side of the mountain, I stop to have my lunch. Today's offering is the Grand Cuvée of mountain food, a tin of Soldatensart Bonersuppe. A hunter green label wraps a surprisingly heavy can. Inside is a thick mash of bean and ham stew, the same off-white color as freezer-burned vanilla ice cream. I clear a space among the rocks and set up my little Esbit stove. Soon the bitter reek of fuel-tablet smoke is wisping up into my face.

When the stew is done, I settle back out of the wind, mess tin clutched in my fingerless-gloved hands, and stare out across the glacier.

The borderline between the world of stone and the world of ice is absolute. You step from one onto the other. There is nothing in between. The ice is hypnotic. After hours of clambering over these boulders, I want to run out over the smooth surface of the glacier, which arcs down into the valley beyond. From where I sit, the eastern face of Smorrstabbtinden rises hundreds of feet, leaning out over the glacier and shadowing its lower reaches with a darkness almost like night.

I shudder, knowing I almost got myself killed up there. What was that strange madness that made me want to keep climbing? I have never felt it before. Even though it only passed through me a short while ago, I can no longer recall how it felt. All that remains is the fear.

An image appears in my head of clinging to that slope, but not through my own eyes. It is as if I am standing off to one side, seeing myself. And then I realize with a shock that the image is not of me. It is of a dead man, clothes torn to rags, bones broken, flesh half-peeled away, and that which remains is white as alabaster. It is the body of Robert Leigh-Mallory, whose corpse was discovered on Everest in 1999, by a team sent to determine whether Mallory, and his colleague Andrew Irvine, had reached the summit in 1924, decades before Sir Edmund Hillary and Tensing Norgay's success in 1953.

The details of this story are hammered like nails into my head. As I huddle at the edge of this vast sea of ice, what happened over eighty years ago on the other side of the world seems as real and close as the rocks beneath my feet and Mallory himself as alive as I am now.

He was considered by many mountaineers of the day to be one of the most accomplished climbers in the world. In 1921, and again in 1922, British attempts to reach the top of Everest had failed. The 1922 attempt had cost the lives of seven Sherpas, who were killed in an avalanche. The burden of responsibility for this catastrophe, in as much as there could be any blame for such an act of nature, had fallen to Mallory. On this, his third attempt, he was determined to take no unnecessary risks. And yet the pressure to reach the summit had never been stronger. Mallory was thirty-six, fast approaching the end of his days when summitting Everest could be considered physically possible. He was torn between his beautiful wife, Ruth, and his children and the lure of the mountain that had become his obsession.

Irvine was younger, only twenty-two, straight out of Oxford, where he had excelled at rowing and had won a coveted "Blue." As valuable as his enthusiasm and his physical strength was his ability to fix the poorly designed and cumbersome oxygen apparatus, which the team planned to use on their final climb to the top. Irvine had even redesigned the apparatus and had submitted his new plans to the company that made them, but nothing was done about it. Once the expedition arrived in India and began to travel cross-country toward Tibet, Irvine was left to rebuild the machinery, using what primitive tools he could scrounge up. By the time they reached the foothills of Everest, Irvine had considerably lightened each oxygen-carrying set. Nevertheless, the sets were still heavy, the cylinders still leaked, and the clothing they had available—heavy hobnailed boots, Norfolk jackets, and woolen climbing breeches—inspires both admiration and disbelief in high-altitude climbers of today.

On the morning of June 6, Mallory and Irvine left their camp at 23,180 feet, with the plan of reaching the 29,029-foot summit and returning before dark. They were in what present-day climbers call the Zone of Death. The chances of surviving a night out in the wind and cold are next to none, and those who die out there are usually left by their comrades, whose energies cannot be spared in transporting down the body of someone for whom there is no longer any hope.

Just after noon, they were seen by one of the other expedition climbers, a man named Noel Odell, as they reached a hub of rock known as the Second Step, just eight hundred feet from the summit. Although, by Odell's reckoning, they were late in reaching the Step, the two men were making good time, and he remained confident that Mallory and Irvine would reach their objective.

But that was the last time anyone ever saw Mallory and Irvine alive. Even this sighting was later brought into question, when Odell confessed that he could no longer be certain he had seen the pair at the Second Step. At such an altitude the mind is slow to function. The eyes play tricks. Memory grows faulty.

In 1933, on a subsequent expedition to Everest, an ice ax was found near a rock formation called the First Step, some distance below where Odell said he had seen the two climbers. The ice ax, marked with three precise horizontal cuts, was identified as belonging to Irvine.

In 1979, Chinese climber Wang Hong-bau confided in a fellow climber, Japanese alpinist Yoshinori Hasegawa, that he had, on a previous expedition, found the body of a "dead English," some three thousand feet above the 1924 expedition's final camp. The dead man was wearing old clothing, which disintegrated as it was touched. No more could be learned about this, since Wang Hong-bau died in an avalanche the day after he told his story.

Other finds over the years, including one of the oxygen cylinders, served to keep alive the mystery of Mallory's and Irvine's last day alive.

Most tantalizing of all was the belief that Irvine had been carrying a camera, which he would certainly have used to document their reaching of the summit, had they reached their objective. If the camera had survived on Irvine's body, the film might, given the cold climate, still be developable.

It was this camera the 1999 crew had come to find. Guiding them was a computer model produced by a young German named Jochen

Hemmleb. Although he had never even been to Everest, his interest in the mystery was such that he had, he believed, calculated the place where Mallory's and Irvine's bodies would most likely have ended up, had they fallen off the side of the mountain.

To say that Hemmleb's theory was met with initial skepticism would be a wild understatement, but such was the interest in solving the mystery, and so precise and compelling were Hemmleb's calculations, that an expedition was mounted by veteran Everest expedition leader Eric Simonson, along with some of the finest climbers in the world, to put Hemmleb's theory to the test.

Hemmleb had the search team looking farther down the mountain than Wang Hong-bau's sighting. Amazingly, his calculations proved correct. Heading out across the steeply sloping terrain beneath Everest's famous Yellow Band, American climber Conrad Anker discovered the bodies of many other climbers who had tumbled off the mountain to their deaths. Most were mangled by their falls, and datable by the gear they were still wearing. Then Anker spotted the body of a man wearing what remained of much earlier clothing than the others. He lay facedown on the gravel incline, his frozen body still gripping the slope. One of his legs had been broken in the fall, and he had suffered a severe head injury that Anker likened to someone having been hit by a hammer. Summoning the other members of the team who had taken part in searching the area, they initially assumed that they had come across the body of Andrew Irvine. Upon further investigation, they realized from name tapes on the body's clothing that they had in fact located Mallory himself. On Mallory's body they found letters, matches, snow goggles, even food, all in an almost perfect state of preservation. But no camera. If Wang Hong-bau's story holds true, the other "dead English" he saw at 26,575 feet must have been that of Irvine, whose exact location remains a mystery.

In one sense, whether Mallory and Irvine reached the summit is academic. As Hillary correctly pointed out, the point is not only to reach the top of the mountain but to get back down again as well.

To me, Mallory and Irvine mark the end of an era. Having not taken part in the race for the North Pole, and having failed in the race for the South Pole, the British were determined to claim Everest, the "third pole." In their failure Mallory and Irvine represent, as much in their deaths as in life, the spirit of the British Empire. Exhausted by the human cost of World War One, it had already begun to crumble.

I do not mourn the empire, but I feel the loss of some of the heroes it produced. The worst thing you could say about the kind of schools I went to in England was that they prepared us for a world that no longer existed. We lived, for better and worse, by the same codes as these men who perished in their search for glory. But the world that waited for us outside had no use for such heroes anymore, and we were forced to relearn much of what we had once thought were absolutes.

For me there is another lesson in that macabre transposing of my own body onto the frozen corpse of Mallory. It is the lure of the mountains themselves. Since I first walked out into these hills, I have drifted back and forth between the hard task of climbing and the mythic world these mountains represent. Somewhere between the solidity of these rocks and the dreams they inspire, there may be, as in the valley at Brangsdalen, some band of life we have not learned to see. But there is also death. You see it in the scattered bones of sheep and reindeer, and you try to ignore it. You feel it in the burning of adrenaline when a rock slides out from under you and you just manage to avoid tumbling off some nameless precipice. You can smell it in your own sweat, which when brought about by fear smells different than it does from pure exertion. You think it will not come for you, that your luck will hold out. But sooner or later, you are made aware of the appalling fragility of flesh in places like this.

I think about a man named Joe Wood, whom I knew at Yale. He disappeared while hiking up on Mount Rainier. He was last seen by a climber who was coming down the mountain. On learning of his disappearance, several of Joe's friends flew out to Washington to search for him, but turned up nothing. Rangers at the park believed he might have fallen through an ice bridge and been swept away down an underground river.

Despite the residue of fear Joe's death has left in my mind, I can still hear the echo of that madness that has told me to keep going up the mountain. I wonder if Mallory felt it, too. I think he must have.

Turning my back on Smorstabbtinden, I set my sights on the nearby peak of Storbreatinden. First I have to climb down along the ridge, or col, which joins the two mountains. I cross a ledge of ice, which hangs above the rock like a half-closed lid on a trunk. Water drips from the sharp edge of the overhang, and here I fill my cup and drink. From there, up the side of Storbreatinden, the climb goes easily.

I soon find myself on a narrow slice of rock, perhaps only ten feet wide, with thousand-foot drops on either side. At the bottom of each side lies a glacier, Storbrean to the south and Veslbrean to the north. Veslbrean is flecked with dirty silt, but Storbrean's ice is polished and clean, painful to my eyes without goggles to soften the glare. Out there on the snowfields, the wind stirs up miniature white tornadoes. I take a stone the size of my head and hurl it out toward Storbrean, but it is so far down that I cannot see it hit the ground. This is no place to linger. One hard gust of wind would blow me off the edge. It is already late in the day, and I have a long way to go before I reach the cozy wooden box of my room at the Krossbu lodge.

I climb down in the marmalade light of sunset. Lichen glows like splashes of molten lava on the rocks. The stones slip and grind beneath my feet, some with sounds like crockery breaking, others more like safe doors slamming.

In a hollow I find a reindeer antler, jutting like Excalibur from between two shelves of rock. The place is almost totally inaccessible. How a reindeer got here, I cannot guess, unless the antler was dropped someplace above and made its own way down among the drifts of winter snow.

I have never seen a reindeer—pictures of them, of course, but never a real one—and what I have read leads me to believe I am unlikely to spot one in the Jotunheimen. During the summer they retreat into the hinterland, although how much more "hinter" you can get than this I do not know. Only in winter do they make their way down toward the valleys. I might have better luck in another area of wilderness called the Dovrefjell, which is also home to a herd of muskoxen. I have never seen one of those, either, and am not even completely sure what one looks like. So right then I decide to visit the Dovrefjell, once I have taken care of business here in the Jotunheimen, and track down the owners of these lightning bolts of bone.

By the time I arrive, the sun has gone and the air is smoked with twilight. Dinner is just being served. Without time to change, I settle down among the students, crowded elbow to elbow at the long wooden tables. They are just in from the mountains, too. I see the white dust of dried sweat in the corners of their eyes and can feel it in my own.

At the other end of the room, Carlsson and Hellborg are holding court. The way their hands twist in the air, showing how they scaled the mountains, they remind me of pictures I have seen of fighter pilots, showing the dogfights they won up in the sky. Everyone is exhausted but happy. Carlsson and Hellborg's gift of bringing them to this place is beyond all price. To see the proof of this in the faces of these students, it is no wonder that the two men keep coming back year after year, to this place at the end of the world.

Chapter Ten

"The Englishman Is Mad"

As Tjernagel made his way up onto the high ground beyond Krossbu, he wrote that "an unaccountable depression of spirits assailed me and the scenery, which is described as the wildest in Norway, wore for me a frowning look."

The landscape is certainly wild. The twenty-kilometer stretch of road that passes through here took two hundred workers two years to build, and has been open to cars only since 1939. In Tjernagel's day, you went on horseback or, as he did, on foot. There are no trees, only banks of snow and rock, even the smallest of which shows signs of having been scraped and gouged and crushed by the movement of glaciers. You can't help imagining that this is what the whole country must have looked like ten thousand years ago, when the last ice age receded, revealing the scarred earth and luring the first humans out into its wilderness. In many lakes, chunks of ice drift at the mercy of the scudding wind, and the deep blue color of the water seems to promise depths that reach down to the burning belly of the Earth.

Not far out of Krossbu, I pass the lonely Sognefjellshytte. Cut into the crossbeam of the lodge's doorway is a cross. The carving is beautiful in its simplicity, placed there to ward off unchristian spirits, of which history had recorded more than a few up here.

Along the snaking road toward the lodge at Turtagro, I pass the infamous Galgeberg. These hills were once the hunting ground of a band of thieves who so terrorized people seeking to pass from the lowlands of the Sognefjord into the countryside around Lom that eventually the locals took matters into their own hands. They caught the robbers, hanged them, and then threw their bodies off the Galgeberg cliff.

Tjernagel did not meet robbers, but he did encounter "some rather stiff people from England, whose garb and demeanor showed them to be gentlefolk of the correctest pattern. Here in the mountain wilderness, I dare say, one is apt to rub elbows with more of the elect of that country than if one were to walk up and down the Strand or Piccadilly for an hour. The Norwegian snow-fields form, in summer, a meeting-place for them."

I can't help wondering if Tjernagel had just met Mr. W. C. Slingsby, whose name is still spoken with admiration in this corner of the world and with no greater reverence than at Turtagro.

Just when you are beginning to wonder if the person who built this road designed it with the intention of killing anyone who dared to drive on it, you arrive at the overlook of Oscarshaug, where King Oscar of Sweden, and in those days of Norway too, paid a visit in 1860. Before you stretches the Helgedalen valley, dominated by the most imposing mountain in the entire Jotunheimen. It is the Skagastoltindane. What makes this mountain famous is not its height (it ranks at eighth tallest in Norway) but the appalling severity of its slopes. Until 1876, when a certain "mad Englishman" came along, not only had no one ever climbed Skagastoltindane, but it was thought that no one ever could.

Two hotels used to perch here, in the crook of this steep and grassy valley. One was the Oino Hotel, where Tjernagel stayed because it was the "least pretentious of the two." The other is the Turtagro Hotel, which in its "pretentiousness" seems to have outlasted the competition, as the Oino no longer exists.

I see nothing pretentious about Turtagro. The hotel is of a modern design, sharply roofed as if to mimic the mountains themselves. Large, irregular windows are sectioned the way ice forms in a pond. As I climb the wide stone steps to the entrance, I see that it is not only new in design, but, in fact, still under construction. Bulldozers are parked out back, and the ground is opened up to reveal a network of pipes.

At the reception desk, a man with shoulder-length blond hair explains what happened to the lodge that once stood here. A fire broke out the year before, when the lodge was closed for the winter. The alarm was hooked up to the nearest fire department, forty kilometers away in Lustra, but because no one was here to fight the flames, by the time the fire crew arrived from the nearest town, the building had burned to the ground.

I think back to the Krossbu lodge, with its century of wood smoke steeped into the walls, its lopsided furniture and picture gallery of guests. If Turtagro was anything like Krossbu, they lost much more than any new structure could replace.

Slumped on a couch just inside the door is a young man of college age. At first, I mistake his vacant stare for physical exhaustion, but then I realize that the look on his face is more one of dejection. My mind races off on the assumption that there is bad weather coming. He has traveled all the way from Oslo, only to learn that the Skagastoltindane and its slightly less fear-inspiring neighbor, Dyrhaugsryggen, both of which are clearly visible from the foyer of the lodge, are soon to be blanketed in snow. I nod a commiserating hello and am surprised when he greets me in English. It turns out that his downcast face has nothing to do with the weather that, on the contrary, is projected to be good. He is an American student from Georgia, who has spent the summer giving kayak lessons on the Sognefjord, which lies only twenty kilometers away at the bottom of the valley. He mumbles something about it not being what he expected.

"Well, at least you've got the mountains to climb," I say cheerfully.

He gives me a withering stare. "It wasn't my idea to come up here," he says. He then goes on to explain how he had agreed to act as mountain guide for another American whom he met down on the fjord.

"How did it go?" I ask.

The college boy shakes his head. "The old guy almost died. He was so unprepared." A sigh trails from his lungs. "So unprepared."

At that moment, the American appears. He is in his fifties, thin and graying, and wears a set of bright yellow plastic bib overalls with an oversized blue plastic raincoat. The college boy is right enough that if the man went climbing in this gear, he really was unprepared. Even Tjernagel's calfskin shoes and wool overcoat would be better than overalls more suited for the deck of a trawler.

The Old Guy is trying to secure a room for a lower price, but the blond-haired man behind the desk politely informs him that all the rooms will be booked up by that evening. It is a Friday, and many climbers are traveling up from Oslo to take advantage of what will most likely be the last good weather of the season. "If you want to save some money," says the blond-haired man, "it is OK if you sleep on the floor in the hallway of the older building." He gestures toward a separate structure located farther up the hill. It is a large two-story house, brick red with white gingerbread latticework, from which it is possible to guess at the charm of the building that burned down.

Behind the Old Guy's back, College Boy rolls his eyes. He raises his hands and lets them fall again, then sinks back even further into the couch.

I feel bad for him. He himself does not look equipped for mountain climbing, and to guide a person even less prepared is more than anyone should do. I think about Hemingway's story "The Short Happy Life of Francis Macomber," in which a safari guide leads a husband and wife on a hunting expedition in Africa. The husband, Francis Macomber, proves to be a coward. His wife ends up sleeping with the guide, and makes no particular secret of it. Macomber is ultimately able to retrieve his self-respect, but only in the moment of his death. Well before this, the guide knows that the trip has gone to hell. He talks about how, when guides meet each other out on the plains, and ask each other how their trips are going, one guide might tell the other that he is "still drinking their whiskey." That is a sign that the trip has gone bad.

This College Boy is still drinking the Old Guy's whiskey, so to speak, but for how much longer I don't know.

Old Guy seems well aware of College Boy's opinions, even though I doubt the College Boy has spelled them out. The Old Guy's forced smile flickers on and off his face. He seems torn between continuing with another day of mountaineering, and perhaps salvaging the trip, or throwing in the towel and heading back down the mountain. I feel bad for him, too. A thing like this can cast a shadow over your entire journey, so that, when the memories have settled in your brain, all of them linger in the gloom of this one part of the trip gone to hell.

They choose a room in the old building and head out. The trailing cuffs of Old Guy's overalls rustle over the stone.

The blond-haired man and I watch them go. Then we turn to each other and sigh.

Given the choice between one of the new rooms and one in the older building out back, I choose the older. With a single swinging motion and an involuntary grunt, I hoist my pack and head outside again.

The older house is built upon a pedestal of rock, on which it seems to have swooned, with the result that there is barely one straight line in its construction. It has, over the years, settled into an architectural craziness like something out of an Escher print. But having settled, the building exudes an air of proud solidity, as if the mountains have tried to evict it and failed.

Inside is a dark and floorboard-creaking hallway on which hang pictures of the glory days of climbing in these mountains. And there, grinning from a faded black-and-white portrait, is the man whose story drew me to this place, the ultimate "mad Englishman." William Cecil Slingsby.

Of all my deceased traveling companions on this journey, Slingsby is the most accomplished. That is to say, he did not merely wander in these mountains, as I and the others have done. Slingsby was a pioneering member of the society of climbers which reached their zenith in the mid-1920s, along with men like Mallory and Irvine, Noel Odell and Geoffrey Winthrop Young, the dashing ex-master at Eton, who left his post after allegations of liaisons with his students. Pictures of Young show a dashing, mustached man wearing a beret and smoking a pipe. Young cultivated an admiring friendship with Mallory, even going so far as to pay his expenses on a climbing trip to the Alps that the two men made in 1909.

Mallory was famously handsome and had many admirers in what was known as the Bloomsbury Set. These included the aggressively flirtatious Strachey brothers, who dubbed their time with Mallory "L'affaire George" and seem to have delighted in broadcasting their conquests.

On Everest, Mallory left them all behind. I can't help wondering if some small part of Mallory's participation in those dangerous, and ultimately fatal expeditions was to retrieve the self-respect he might have lost in the gossip machine of his Oxford days.

Many of the participants in these mountaineering adventures were Oxford or Cambridge men. As such, there was an element of snobbery to these early mountaineering societies, and the failure of the first two British attempts at Everest was, in Mallory's own estimation, due in part to the fact that the expedition members were chosen because of where they stood socially rather than how well they could climb. Many were too old and too unfit. This was proven out by the fact that in 1921 the leader of the expedition, Alexander Kellas, died of exhaustion before even reaching the mountain.

The snobbery extended not only to who was climbing but also where they chose to climb. At the time Norway was not considered to be a place for serious mountaineers. The peaks were considered too low, and the Alps were much preferred. The real problem with Norwegian mountains lay in the fact that their potential was simply unknown. Slingsby changed all that. He was, over a period ranging from 1872 to 1921, the first climber to explore the high ranges and as such became rightly known as the Father of Norwegian Mountaineering. He is even credited as having introduced the sport of skiing to Norway, elevating it above a simple means of getting around. Proof of his accomplishments is the fact that three sections of Skagastolstind are actually named after him. Also, in 1921, Slingsby was received by King Haakon himself and was treated as a royal personage in almost every town he passed through on his way into and out of the mountains.

Slingsby's account of his adventures, titled *Norway, The Northern Playground*, was first published in Edinburgh in 1904. Given his contribution to the sport of mountaineering, I expected the book would still be in print when I first went looking for it. No such luck. The only copies I could find were first editions, none costing less than a thousand dollars a piece. Thanks to Greg Glade of Top of the World Books in Vermont, I was able to purchase a 1941 reprint that was part of a mountaineering library series. Even that cost more than the books of all my other companions combined. The truth is, I was lucky to find a copy at all.

This points toward a strange discrepancy in how these various men are remembered. Three in Norway can be found in almost every bookshop in the country, but the rest are largely forgotten. The answer lies in their readability. I liked the stories of Lees and Clutterbuck, as well as that of Williams, right from the start. Simpson I grew to like. Baynes was in such a hurry that I never got to know him. Tjernagel, with his Monty Python-esque approach to mountaineering, I enjoyed for reasons that would certainly have left him feeling indignant. Some of Slingsby's writing, on the other hand, is too technical to be compelling unless you have a working knowledge of the mountains he describes. The reason for this is simply that he did not write for people like me, but rather for mountaineering colleagues like Geoffrey Young, who penned an introduction for the 1941 reprint.

Not only was Slingsby less of a snob than his contemporaries about the mountains of Norway, he was also a great admirer of Norwegians. This included Ole Berge, owner of the Turtagro Hotel, who accompanied him on several climbs. Slingsby's narrative shows a refreshing lack of condescending remarks about "masculine women" and "idiot" mountain folk. The reason he felt so comfortable with the Norwegians was because, as he rightly pointed out, his ancestors came from this country. Slingsby was a Yorkshireman. Yorkshire, and much of northern England, was colonized by Norwegian Vikings, who left a legacy that endures not only in the physical appearance of the "Dales" people, but in much of the language that is specific to northern England. You only have to watch a rerun of All Creatures Great and Small to pick up this ancient vernacular.

The fundamental temperament of Norwegians strongly appealed to Slingsby; qualities of straightforwardness, honesty, and love of the outdoors that I have also come to admire.

My home for the next two days, a small but tall-ceilinged room at the far corner of the building, opens out onto a balcony where a group of climbers are noisily celebrating their escape from the city. Their crampons, ropes, ice axes, and helmets are piled against the railing.

I dump my pack and flop spread-eagled onto the bed, noticing as I fall yet another picture of Slingsby directly above my pillow. In this one he is poised at the top of a mountain, a soft cap on his head and breeches tucked into knee socks. He is leaning on a long ice ax, smiling a triumphant smile.

A moment later, I hear some muttering close by. Looking up, I see two of the celebrating climbers peering through the window at me. They look concerned, guessing perhaps from my posture on the bed that I have expired. Through bleary eyes I blink at them. As soon as they realize I am still alive, they get flustered and turn away. I expect these are part of the Oslo crowd. They look like city folk, snappily dressed in tight jeans and Dale sweaters, fast-talking in a way that sets them apart from the people I've grown used to seeing since I made my way up into the hills.

With only a short time before I head back to Oslo, my mind drifts toward the comforts of urban life. I tell myself it might be nice to see a movie, to walk anonymous among the crowds, to feel the constant rolling thunder of a city. More importantly, I am anxious to set right some of the misconceptions about Norway and the Norwegians that I have carried with me since childhood.

Still hovering at the back of my mind is a stereotype of Norwegians as the descendants of ax-wielding barbarians, but this ancient image clashes wildly with the gentleness, honesty and generosity of the Norwegians I have met on my journey.

I must confront this country's past in a way that merges with the present, rather than conflicts with it. My chance to do that, I believe, does not lie out here but in an Olso museum devoted to the culture of the Vikings and the boats that brought them to the farthest reaches of the known world.

In this region of snow and ice, another matter has returned to haunt me. It is an imagined picture of Captain Scott, frozen to death in his tent. I do not think about why he failed in his mission to be the first at the South Pole as much as I wonder why Amundsen succeeded. Was it simply bad luck that killed Scott, or was there something in the two cultures, the British and the Norwegian, which caused the men to tackle the same problem differently? And, if so, why did the culture that raised me fail so miserably? In Oslo's Holmenkollen Ski Museum, where the artifacts of Amundsen's voyage are on permanent display, I mean to find some answers.

These two cultures, twined by ancient blood, were more recently entwined during the Second World War. After the debacle of Mauriceforce and the British retreat from Andalsnes, Norway lived for almost five years under the boot of Nazism. Much of Britain's modern sense of self, and America's too, is defined by those war years. In the Hjemmefrontmuseet war museum, I hope to catch a glimpse of how that time lives on in the Norwegian consciousness.

These three facets of history, which once comprised almost everything I knew about Norway, linger distortedly in my mind, demanding resolution. The more I think about it, the more I realize I might be hoping for too much from these museums. The relics they contain may not speak to me the way I need them to, but only seeing them will tell.

I get up to draw the curtains and notice, as I near the window, the Old Guy and the College Boy lugging their gear back to their car. They do not talk, and seem in a hurry to leave. They hurl their gear into the back of a beaten-up white station wagon and spin their wheels in the dirt leaving the parking lot. I watch the white car growing smaller as it disappears down into the valley.

College Boy must have spoken his mind, and the Old Guy called it quits. It would take more than whiskey to put things right between those two now.

By the time I make it over to the main lodge, hoping to scrounge up some dinner, the place is packed. Expensive cars crowd the parking lot and guests are drifting in and out of the dining room, drinks in hand.

At the reception desk, I introduce myself to Ole Berge Draegni, great-grandson of the Ole Berge who knew Slingsby. He is very tall, with blue and patient eyes, which is just as well, since he is now besieged from all directions with inquiries about the weather, about rooms, about dinner. Through this, Ole Berge remains entirely unflustered. When I ask him about whether there is a marked trail up the mountain known as Dryhaugsryggen, he spots the name Slingsby in my notebook and his eyes light up. "What do you know about Slingsby?" he asks.

I mention the book.

He nods and rises from his seat, but then sits back down again with a sad look on his face. "I forgot," he said. "It was destroyed in the fire. Often now I go to look for a book and have to remind myself that it is no longer there."

I don't know what to say. The loss for him, as part of a chain that stretches back four generations, must still be overwhelming.

"There is a book about it," he says.

"About what?" I ask.

"A book about Slingsby's book."

Now it is my eyes that light up.

He leads me into a room with glass cases, couches, and tables. The shelves in the cases are mostly empty, but a few old volumes mark the beginning of a new library, which may one day replace the one he lost.

The book, written by Jan Schwarzott, is, unfortunately, in Norwegian. I ask Ole Berge if there is a translation in English. He shakes his head. Not here and not anywhere, further proof of Slingsby's displaced fame. Even though the language is beyond me, I can see the exhaustive research that has gone into it. It is considerably longer than the original. Every page of the original text has been exhaustively annotated, and pictures found for every person mentioned. There is even the logo of the Yorkshire Ramblers Club, of which Slingsby was a prominent member. But there is only so much I can decipher. It is frustrating. I imagine this is what it must feel like to be dyslexic. The words are all there, all half-familiar from my years of studying German, but I just can't quite make sense of them. Accepting defeat, I return the book to the shelf and shuffle in to a dinner of roast lamb and boiled potatoes.

IN THE MIDDLE OF THE NIGHT, I am jolted from my sleep by the sound of monstrous snoring, the kind of gargling, honking, backward flatulence for which trolls would normally be blamed.

The walls of the old building are thin, evidently, but I don't know how much help thicker walls would be against such snarling. On my way to the bathroom, I trip over the culprit, a man wrapped in a sleeping bag and wedged up against my door like a rolled-up carpet. Along the hallway are several others, cocooned in mummy bags. In the moonlight, I catch sight of distant Skagastolstind as the wind whips up a cloud of snow from its summit. It looks like a huge reptile shedding its skin.

I wake before dawn, but the sleepers in the hall are already gone. After a breakfast of porridge and coffee, I strike out for the mountains. The narrow, well-trodden route snakes along the floor of a valley called Skarstoldsbotn. The ground is lush with grass and bluish-purple flowers. They are called turt in Norwegian, and it is for these that Turtagro is named.

The path soon begins to climb steeply, passing several pools of swirling green water. I no longer feel the pain of exertion. I sweat, and the going is hard, but I do not gasp for breath and feel the burning in my muscles as I did when I climbed Storronden, what seems like lifetimes ago.

Having learned my lesson at Krossbu, I will not attempt to climb Skagastolstindane, or even a part of it. The razorback that forms the northern ridge, high up on my left, rises and falls like the musical notes of a mad opera. Those are ice ax–climbing slopes, daggers-in-your-boots crampon-climbing slopes. As Slingsby made his way up the same valley I am climbing now, he saw many traces of bear, which had recently nibbled the tops off Angelica plants growing beside the path. Both his guide, Knut Lykken, and a climbing companion named Mohn were stopped five hundred feet beneath the summit by a rock wall that Slingsby described as "nearly perpendicular and almost entirely without ledges ... it is difficult to imagine any mountain presenting a more impractical appearance than is shown at first sight by this peak."

Neither Mohn nor Lykken would go on. Mohn called an ascent "perfectly impossible." Lykken, who has already prophesied earlier that "the Englishman is mad. He will kill himself," said simply, "I shall not risk my life there." This was an exception to Slingsby's maxim that "an English tourist in the Jotunheimen can indulge in any eccentricities he likes without exciting much remark."

So Slingsby went on alone, up five hundred feet of almost vertical rock. His friends tried to call him back, but he kept going. "Three times I was almost beaten, but this was my especial and longed-for mountain."

At last, on the peak, in full view of his comrades down below, he raised a cheer that echoed out across the valley. He stood at a precipice that fell away four thousand feet to an ice-choked lake below. "It would be futile for me to describe it," he said of the view. It was a moment he described as "silent worship."

Leaving what Slingsby called "the grisly towers" of Skagastol-stindane, I turn west, crossing the fast-running river that sluices from the Skardstolsbreen glacier, and begin to climb the neighboring mountain of Dyrhaugsryggen. The sound of the river fades away behind me. Then there is only the wind, snuffling through the grass and across the dirty banks of snow left over from the winter.

There is no path up this mountain. You just climb it. At first this doesn't seem like too hard a task. From below, Dyrhaugsryggen seems almost gentle in its ascent. A postcard that is sold at Turtagro makes the slope look almost too easy to bother with.

What you don't see in the postcard is that the boulders on the slope above the grass line are the size of small cars, each one of which has to be scrambled over. The slope is also ridged with deep gullies, which you have to climb down into and then up again.

In one of these gullies I find a red emergency sled for transporting bodies down the mountain. The sled has either been abandoned, lost, or set aside. I can't tell which. It is a sobering thing to discover, especially when you are alone.

The top third of the mountain is covered in snow, which I find much easier to climb than the rocks. I jab my toes in through the icy crust, making steps on my way up. The sun is out. Soon I am stripped down to my shirt, and my snow goggles are steaming up with sweat.

The climb is so steep that my face is only a couple of feet from the snow. I can't tell where the summit lies. The ground bulges out like the belly of a sleeping giant.

When I stop and turn, the steepness of the slope makes me dizzy. I drink the last of the water in my canteen, then pack it full of snow and keep climbing. Miniature tornadoes of snow spin along the crest of the ridge, vanishing into the blue.

By the time I reach the ridge, my heartbeat is pulsing in my neck. There, only a few feet beyond a clump of rocks, the ground disappears. I scrabble as close to the edge as I dare, peering at Fremste Skarstolvatnet Lake, three thousand feet below. Beyond it, the seemingly endless expanse of the Styggedal, Gjertvass, and Maradals glaciers fan out blindingly beneath the cloudless sky. My map runs out long before I reach the limits of the view. From the top of Skagastolstindane, on a climb twenty-four years after his first summitting of the mountain, Slingsby clearly saw a mountain called the Folgefonni, one hundred and twenty miles distant.

With my sweat already cooling, I struggle into my clothes and swallow a bite of stale crispbread. It tinkles down my throat like shards of broken glass, but I would still rather have this than Slingsby's hiking menu of deviled tongue, Chicago corned beef (whatever that is), and a pipe full of tea leaves to smoke afterward.

Skagastolstindane is so close across the narrow valley and seems so out of scale that I feel as if I could reach across and, with one gentle sweep of my hand, level off its shark-teeth ridges as one might on a sandcastle at the beach.

Lying back in the snow, I fill my eyes with the hazy, whiskey-colored light filtering in through my goggles. The pain in my muscles ebbs away. My heartbeat slows. My breathing comes even and deep.

In this moment, I realize something that changes my entire journey.

For each mountain I have climbed, I have in fact been climbing two. There is the mountain made of snow and rock, and there is the mountain in my head—the thing that the mountain stands for, the competition with myself, the clarity of thought that comes from climbing.

But suddenly these two overlapping mountains have come together, creating a balance of the mental and the physical that before I could only experience individually, swaying back and forth between the world of the mind and the world of my thundering heart. Now I feel them both at the same time.

Having finally abandoned all hope of figuring it out, the great indescribable emotion experienced by all of my companions has appeared in front of me. I understand now that the reason for its being indescribable is not because the words don't exist, but because it's almost impossible to figure out what the emotion actually is. That "indescribable thing" is the profound experience of living completely in the present.

This is the meaning of Slingsby's "silent worship." He wrote that, in the years that lay ahead, the moment never grew dull. It remained always clear, as if it were still happening. Because it *was* still happening. That moment was *always* the present, unbuckling the fetters of time.

Why this should happen to me now, I do not know. I have climbed harder before, have seen views just as grand. I was not thinking about this when I climbed. It is almost like when I figured out how to swim. I struggled with it for ages, half-drowning in the shallow end of pools. And then, just when I was about to give up, I discovered I could do it. I remember perfectly the moment when everything suddenly worked, and I did not have to fight against it, or even think about it anymore.

When Slingsby reached the summit of Skagastolstindane, he pinned a handkerchief under a stone, which was seen through a telescope by people back at Turtagro. What a grand and visible conquest his was on that day, and what a quiet, invisible thing I have to show for my own climb. But I would not trade it for the world.

By the time I make it back to Turtagro, the other climbers have moved on and the hotel is not as crowded. No one will have to sleep on the floor tonight. I eat a quiet supper in a room turned sepia with sunset, then squelch back through the mud to my room in the lop-sided house. I fall into a peaceful, dreamless sleep, soaring through the darkness, like a man who has learned how to fly.

Chapter Eleven

In Love with Matilda

AT THE END OF A LONG, MURDEROUSLY NARROW ROAD ALONG
the east bank of the Lustrafjorden stands the ancient church of Urnes.

I almost didn't come here. I was bound for the Dovrefjell, having
gotten it in my head that I must see a reindeer, and a muskox, too,
whatever that is. But then, coming down out of the mountains on the
road from Turtagro, I began to wonder why I should be in such a hurry.
I was reentering a world of trees and tall grass and meadow flowers,
which seemed impossibly lush after days up on the tundra.

Tjernagel walked this road, which took him "into many a corner,
made many seemingly purposeless twists and turns, dropped into
hidden crevices, but never lost itself, always finding a way out." Houses
stood so close to the road that he "could have laid hands on the crown
of the venerable grandfather as he sat by the open window sipping
his afternoon coffee."

In a strange echo of that moment, I pass by what must be that
same house and see what must be the grandson of that "venerable

grandfather" puffing a pipe and reading the paper as he sits beside his open window. The man's gray and wispy hair hangs around his head like a wreath of smoke. His sweater is done up with buttons made of horn.

The house is a pale and cheerful blue, like a clear sky in winter. Lace curtains are pulled back to let in the sun. The front door opens practically onto the road, and the steps turn sharply to the left to avoid ushering people straight into the path of passing cars.

At the bottom of the hill, the Lustrafjorden stretches between steep mountains on either side, its surface less like water than a stretch of sky, as if these mountains do not hug the Earth but jut out into space.

At the town of Fortun, I see a sign for the Urnes church. My plan was to spend the whole day driving in a wide arc to the north and west, around Jostedalsbreen National Park, swing east, and by nightfall reach the Dovrefjell, which forms the tip of a slightly lopsided triangle made up of the Rondane, Dovrefjell, and Jotunheimen wildernesses.

What is the rush? I ask myself. It is not as if I have a scheduled meeting with these reindeer, and if there are any to be found at all, they are not going to vanish between tomorrow and today. Besides, this is the Urnes church, whose picture can be found in almost every art history book ever printed. If I drive by this now, I know I will regret it later.

Regret visits me slightly sooner than expected, however, when I swing around a curve in the road and have to jam on the brakes before I crash into a car coming from the other direction. The road is not wide enough for two cars. It is really just a horse track that has been paved over. But none of the other cars are taking this into account. They simply veer out of the way and then swerve back onto the road.

My deodorant blows out almost audibly after the second of these close encounters. From then on, sweating hands gripping the wheel,

I surrender to the state of mind the locals here must have adopted long ago, which is simply to hope for the best. No bloody wonder they built a church at the end of this road. I expect they had to bury half the people who came to visit.

The houses along the way are hunched beside the road upon this tiny lip of level ground before the mountains blast into the sky. In between the houses are orchards of apple trees, with giant apples, some the size of grapefruit, crowding the branches. I think about my own apple trees in my garden up in Maine. One grows bright red apples, which dot the green canopy of the tree like drops of blood. Another grows pale yellow-green apples, which the deer come for each morning just before sunrise. When I come down in the autumn mornings to light the fire in the stove, there are always one or two deer chomping on the apples that have fallen in the night.

These Lustrafjorden apples are like a cross between the two kinds in my garden. They are the biggest I have ever seen, and when I see a sign for fresh apple juice being sold at a mini-mart up ahead, I decide to stop and buy some.

I zoom past a lay-by, in which stands what looks like an abandoned Coke machine, and it is several seconds before I realize that this *was* the mini-mart.

Marts don't get much more mini than this.

In the small display case are several different-size plastic bottles filled with honey-colored apple juice, and a small box in which to put the money. As my coins rattle into the little wooden box, which has no lock, I am reminded once again that I do not live in a part of the world where little wooden change boxes are secure. I drink half of it straight away. It is sharp and sweet, and I can feel the sugar sparking along the branches of my nerves.

A little farther up the road, I buy an armful of apples from an old woman wearing a shawl and ankle-length skirt. She bears a striking resemblance to the drawing of Marit, the woman Tjernagel encountered when he arrived at the ruins of his old family homestead. Her face is so wrinkled that she even looks like an apple left over from the year before. It is as if the apples have decided to cut humans out of the business and are now growing and selling themselves.

Careening on down the road, I sink my teeth into one of the apples, while the rest roll off the passenger seat at the next sharp corner and bounce around in the seat well. The flesh of the apples is soft, a little pulpy, almost like a mouthful of applesauce. They have the same texture as my apples up in Maine after they have gone mealy. Except these do not taste mealy. These alone were worth the detour, and I wonder why I have never seen them for sale before. Perhaps, because of their softness, they do not travel well.

Just before I come in sight of the Urnes church, I pass under a colonnade of trees, in whose watery shadows I observe something so macabre that it is as if I am entering a place of pagan, not of Christian, worship.

Hanging from the branch of a tree is the bloody skin of a deer. Hanging beside it is a dirt-crusted pair of blue workman's overalls, like the shell of a man. It reminds me of a description by Adam of Bremen, who visited the Norse temple at Uppsala in Sweden. There, hanging from the boughs of a huge tree in the grove of the temple, were dozens of bodies, some animal, some human, hanging indiscriminately together.

Unless this is precisely what it seems to be, I cannot fathom what these things are doing here.

Leaving that grim hollow, I drive up a winding slope to a point where the fjord bends like an elbow, redirecting itself toward the south. It is still very far from the sea, but there is a pleasing openness about the location, and I can understand why someone would build a church here, even though people who wanted to worship had to come across from the other side of the fjord, where the bulk of the population seems to have settled.

The Urnes church is a stave structure, like the one in Lom, and some fifty others scattered around the country. But Urnes is the most famous of them all, because it is for this church that the Urnes style is named. The style, which personifies Viking art, is a form of carving, used on wood as well as stone and metal, that shows animals in interwoven patterns, often snakes and dogs with thin bodies and long legs. Sometimes, they are simultaneously biting each other. Among them, twisted like creepers, are floral motifs, as if these animals have become tangled not only in each other's limbs but in a bramble thicket as well.

The Urnes church was built around the year 1050, at a time when the pagan temple at Uppsala, and the pagan religion as well, was far from finished. But the panels that make the Urnes church so well known are said to come from an even earlier structure that once stood upon this spot, perhaps a pagan temple that was knocked down and recycled by the early Christians.

The most striking thing about this pagodalike structure is the color, so black from centuries of the tar, turpentine, and linseed oil emulsion used to preserve the wood that it looks burned like the skin of a marshmallow cooked too long in a campfire.

It is a Saturday afternoon, and the church is closed, but I soon discover that there are holes cut into the walls and doors, which allow me to peer into the cramped space of the church. Vying with the bitter smell of tar emulsion is the snuff of incense dusting the air among the pews.

The Urnes panels are tall and narrow, dizzying to look at with their intricate designs. An extraordinary amount of work must have gone into their construction. I have heard the Urnes style called purely Scandinavian, but others say it owes a debt to much earlier

Roman designs, and also that the Urnes motifs did not reach their peak among the Scandinavians but among the Irish, who carried over the style into their artwork centuries after the Norse had ceased to work with it.

The stave churches say as much to me about the early days of Christianity as they do about the Norse refusal to abandon entirely the older faith that used to flourish here, and still does in many ways.

Stories are still told about the *hulder*, beautiful women identical to humans in every respect except that they have tails. These they try to hide, in hopes of persuading a man to marry them. If they are successful, they then become human themselves. Then there are the *fossegrimen*, musical imps that live in waterfalls, who can be summoned by throwing a leg of lamb into the water on Thursday nights. In mountain lakes live shape-shifting demons named *nokken*. Less dangerous are the *nissen*, elves who live in barns and for whom bowls of rice pudding are set out in wintertime.

Sometimes, the pagan and the Christian world combine, as on Midsummer Night, during the festival of Jonsok, when those who want to can speak with the dead. To accomplish this, you must stand outside your house all night with a handful of dirt on your head and a Bible in your hands. At dawn, the dead will appear before you and you can answer whatever questions you might have about the afterlife.

Another example of this melding of the new and older faith is at Christmas. In order to pay respect to the slaughtered pig, or *jule-grisen*, a toast is made to each of the twenty-five bones in its right front foot. As with many ancient rituals, the exact meaning of this is lost beneath an overlay of Christian thought.

In the same way, these designs on the Urnes church speak to something lost among the rubble of an older time. In the wrestling of limbs and vines and teeth, some urgent story shouts from the cracked and ebony-dark wood. I think about that deer pelt and the dirty overalls, lynched in that tree down the hill. There is a message in these, too, perhaps closer to the panels in its meaning than the church whose name endures because of them.

THE LODGE AT HJERKINN has sheltered people for over a thousand years. King Eystein commissioned Hjerkinn, and other lodges like it, in the twelfth century. They were to provide travelers moving north and south across the inhospitable terrain of the Dovrefjell mountains with some protection against the elements.

In wintertime, not everybody reached the safety of these shelters, and it was the task of the lodge owner to go out in the spring and find the bodies of those who had frozen to death in the snow. So many perished in the area around Hjerkinn that a church and cemetery were built to give their bones a resting place. When the cemetery filled up, the owner of the Hjerkinn lodge built the skulls into the foundations of a new building on his property.

Facts like these, and the statement in one of my guidebooks that the road up from Dombas into the Dovrefjell is "boring," might be enough to steer someone away from this whole region of Norway. But whoever called that road boring should never have come to Norway in the first place.

The Dovrefjell is a brilliance of rivers like molten sapphires, of round and treeless hills that seem, in the antique light of this autumn afternoon, to be made of brown velvet. Between these hills lie open plains that remind me in places of the sierras of the American West. You almost expect the High Plains Drifter to come riding out of the heat haze.

The lodge stands on a bluff overlooking a large lake. Its white walls and red shutters glow in the sunset. The building is new, the old one having suffered the same fate as Turtagro and Gjendebu, burning to the ground in 1990.

Williams trudged all the way here with his wicker backpack and pocket pistol. He found Hjerkinn a "bustling, rather businesslike place," and soon installed himself in the kitchen; "a large wooden hall ... with rich brown smoke-tinted timbers and blazing fire."

What I find here now are pale wood floors and beams offset by black wrought-iron finishings. Woolen carpets hang on the walls, decorated with Nordic motifs that remind me of New Mexican Chimayo blankets. A fire burns on the peis in the corner. The place is busy with guests, who lounge on the couches drinking glasses of honey-colored Ringnes beer. It is a far cry from the ale Williams was served, which he described as "a turbid liquid, of a reddish green color, and from its flavor appears to be an infusion of hay flavored with a bitter decoction of pine knots."

Behind the main building, just as at Turtagro, is an older house set aside for any overflow of guests, of which I am told I am one. The newer section of the lodge has been taken over by some kind of company outing, made up of a group of decidedly un-mountainy-looking people who are frantically puffing away on cigarettes in the courtyard.

You don't see that many people smoking in Norway. It was the first country to ban smoking advertisements in 1975. The joke about Norwegians among the other Scandinavian nations is that they are all absurdly healthy. One joke that I picked up on this subject begins with two Americans having a discussion at the Oslo airport. The first American says that people think all Scandinavians look the same: blond hair, blue eyes, etc. But this American says he can tell them apart. He points to a man and says that one, for example, is a Swede. The other American decides to put this to the test. He goes over to the "Swede" and asks if he is in fact Swedish. "No," replied the man, "I am Norwegian, but I have been sick for a long time."

The healthy complexion of Norwegians is a feature remarked upon by almost everyone who sees them, as far back as the writings of ninth-century Arab emissary Ibn Al-Fadlan. He called them Al-Magus, the "Fire Worshipers" and said of them that they were "tall as date palms, blonde and ruddy."

He would not have said it about these Norwegians. In their faces I see the gray-green haze of years of tobacco use, and the suppleness of their skin replaced by the bull hide of the smoker.

The back building shares with Turtagro an almost dreamlike undulation in its floorboards. Walking down the well-lit corridor is like being in one of those scenes in a movie after the main character has been poisoned with some sleeping potion and the walls are weaving back and forth. But the room is snug, the water hot, the plain bed good enough. There is even a little radio, on which I pick up a few scraps of English after fiddling with the dial. The by-now unfamiliar language twangs across the room, and I immediately switch the thing off. Opening the window, I let the sounds of the Dovrefjell take the place of the radio static. Cow bells tinkle in the distance. Ravens, hidden in the trees, caw and clack their gun-blued beaks.

I decide to take a walk before dinner. Following a well-worn trail up through a wood of stunted white birch, I soon emerge onto the high ground. The uneven, wildflower-speckled terrain reminds me of Wales. There are so many flowers that I finally haul out my underused book of Mountain Flowers. It is not that I ignored the presence of flowers. I just never felt the need to know their names. But now I am introduced to the pink-petaled clusters of Silene acaulis, or moss campion and up ahead, matting the ground, are the claret-red leaves of Arctostaphylos alpina, black bearberry, whose dark blue fruit are white inside, like tiny, unripe plums, and leave no taste but a faint bitterness in the corners of my mouth.

Nothing on the high ground grows above knee height, and most things are no taller than my ankle. Flowers like purple saxifrage, tangled with the tiny suns of snow buttercups, must keep their heads below the knifing wind. My favorite is the arctic bluebell, its flower like a miniature and gaudy lampshade to decorate the dens of nissen elves and fossegrimen imps.

Changing my focus from the minute yellow petals of alpine hawkweed and the violet globes of melancholy thistle, I stand back and see how all the colors together form a tangled rainbow of the northern world.

Another thing I notice now is that the unevenness of the terrain is not entirely natural. In some places, I see what appear to be the gouges of shell craters. In another place, the ground has been cleared in neat squares, as if to form gun pits for artillery. The Dovrefjell lies up against a military training area, but more than practice wars were fought here in the past.

Back in 1718, when Norway and Sweden were at war, all of the lodges were burned in order to deny shelter to the Swedish Army, which was coming down from the north. Despite this, the Swedish commander tried to lead his men through, with the result that they all froze to death.

Here also, in late April 1940, Norwegians fought a rearguard action against advancing German troops. My maps show the German line of advance moving directly up this valley, following the line of the railroad as it branches from Dombas, one leg heading toward Andalsnes, the other toward Trondheim. I can see the train tracks from here, as well as the tiny Hjerkinn Station, a minute outpost against the vastness of the tundra and the peak of Snohetta mountain in the distance. If the Norwegians were going to attack the advancing Germans, they would have done so from where I am now, with their small mountain guns safely out of the way, just behind the lip of the hill on which I am standing, and artillery spotters directing fire from covered positions on the ridge. This way they would at least have a path of retreat to the east, as it must have been clear to the Norwegians by this stage of the battle for their country that they could not stop the German attack. At best, they would only slow it down enough to allow the British "Paralyzed Polarbears" of Maurice and Sickleforce a chance to escape.

I wonder how the battle went here, whether the Norwegians managed to escape with their guns or if they had to destroy them and run.

The path over these hills is wide and flat. It is an ancient trail, reminding me of the old Roman roads I walked on Dartmoor in the pissing rain and oozing fog in the middle of the night on a particularly nasty cadet maneuver, when we were put at the mercy of 42 Commando, Royal Marines. It was an experience they enjoyed in the exact proportion that we did not.

This road through the Dovrefjell stretches all the way from Oslo to Trondheim. It is a pilgrim's trail, known as the King's Road because of the number of royalty who made the trek to Nidaros, an old name for the city of Trondheim. The marker stones are painted with a red cross, barbed like arrowheads at each end. Woven around the cross is a design like a Celtic knot. On one stone, larger than the rest, the same design is beautifully carved, its rock face polished smooth around the cutting.

I stand back to take a picture of the stone. Just as I am focusing the lens, I see, in the background, two reindeer staring at me. My heart jumps into my throat. Slowly, I lower the camera. They are standing some distance away on a slope covered with pale yellow-green lichen. Their coats are cream except on their back legs, where the fur is brown, but turns white again around the tail. They have heads like deer, only bigger and with broader, blunter snouts and bodies sturdier than deer, bigger around the shoulders. The antlers of this pair are small and fuzzed with velvet, and I think they must be young.

Just as I am raising the camera to my eye again, hoping for a picture, the reindeer get spooked. They bound away over the springy lichen, tails flicked up in alarm. They stop again right at the edge of the next ridge. I can barely see them now, and my lens can't handle the distance. The picture won't amount to much, but I take it anyway.

Shadows stretched by sunset begin to sink below the ground. A haze of twilight settles on the hills. I march back to the lodge, sure that this news will electrify the people there.

I have seen a reindeer!

Dinner is well under way when I arrive. It is a help-yourself arrangement—heaping portions of meatballs with gravy and claret-colored lingonberry jam, salmon and dill sauce, boiled potatoes, flatbread, and something called rommegrot, which I assume is salad dressing and pour onto a side dish of tomatoes.

The waiter eyes me with a look of horror. He waits until I am seated and then comes over.

I have that sinking faux-pas feeling again.

The waiter is a large chap, who seems uncomfortable in his white and black uniform. He does not seem built for this kind of work. I feel a bit envious of Williams, who was waited upon by "the most rosy-cheeked of kitchen maids." Instead, speaking in a quiet voice, the way one man informs another that his fly is undone, my waiter tells me I have made a mistake.

This much I have already guessed.

"That is rommegrot," he says, as if it will explain everything.

I look at him patiently.

He sighs. "Rommegrot is eaten with cinnamon and sugar." He looks around, and then his gaze returns to me. "Not tomatoes!" he hisses.

Dutifully, I return to the food counter, pour some rommegrot into a bowl. It is the color of cream, but thicker, more like a yogurt. Then I sprinkle on some cinnamon and sugar and return to my table.

No sooner have I sat down than the waiter appears again. "No!" he says.

"No?"

"No! You have to eat it with cinnamon, sugar, and sausage!"

"I didn't know about the sausages," I say quietly.

He fetches a plate of salami, then watches while I scoop the rommegrot over the slices.

I look up and smile cautiously.

But he is not smiling.

Carefully, I eat a few slices. My heart thumps in Morse code: "What the hell are you doing to me?"

Now, at last, his crouched-down eyebrows rise, and he is smiling.

"Rommegrot!" I say triumphantly.

"What?" he asks.

"Rommegrot! Didn't I say that right?"

"Not really," he tells me.

But all is not lost. I pull out my trump card. "I saw a reindeer. Up on the hill. Two reindeers actually."

He nods, and if I were not so dead certain that he must be astonished at my news, I would swear he was pitying me. "There are lots of reindeer here," he says. "They are easy to find." With that, he leaves me alone with my bowl of Heart Attack Soup.

My enthusiasm does not stay dampened long. Who cares what the waiter thinks? He lives here, after all. I live in New Jersey, where I recently had to persuade a friend that reindeer actually exist and aren't just a figment of Santa Claus's imagination.

Later, huddled in my sleeping bag in the toast-warm room, I listen to the radio again. Voices fade in and out of the drizzling static, like the muttering of ghosts.

That night, I dream I am getting a tattoo, high up on my left arm. At first I can't see what the tattoo is, but then I see in the mirror that it is the same barbed cross and Celtic knot I found carved on the stone. I actually like it. Maybe I'll get one. You never know.

A muskox, whose picture I discover in a book at Hjerkinn, looks like a very big-headed cow. It has a hump on its shoulders and brown, buffalo-shaggy hair reaching all the way down to its feet. This hair has a vaguely seventies, *Partridge Family* center-parting look to it. The muskox also has horns, narrow and sharp like those of a bull, which swing down in the shape of a J below each ear.

These horns are, I assume, what they use to kill people, a thing they have apparently done more than once since the herd was re-introduced to the Dovrefjell in the early fifties. Other animals had previously been brought in from Greenland, but all of them were killed for food during the war. Thousands of years before that, great herds of muskoxen roamed these hills, but were hunted to extinction. They look like a species that should have vanished from the Earth, along with mammoths and saber-toothed tigers. They have survived by living where few other creatures choose to live, and now maintain an uneasy peace with their human neighbors.

This uneasy peace is made very clear to you on many signs as you walk into the mountains.

Apparently, the muskoxen won't bother you unless you bother them. But you bothering them might not have the same criteria as them deciding to bother you. And them bothering you means running after you at forty miles per hour then poking you with those horns, stepping on you with their nine-hundred-pound bodies and finishing you off with atrociously bad breath.

The best place to stay before you go out and get trampled is at the lodge in Kongsvold. None of my other companions spent the night here, and pity for them, because Kongsvold is one of the most beautifully maintained lodges I have seen. It is a cluster of red- or white-painted buildings: storehouses, living quarters, and a barn, all of which date from between 1700 to 1890. Most of these are facing inward around a central courtyard, very much in the old style. It is the only set of buildings for some distance, close by the road that cuts through the Dovrefjell on its way from Dombas to Trondheim.

Inside, the lodge is a blend of old and new. The wide-plank floor of the sitting room is padded with Persian carpets, and the ceiling is ridged with exposed beams. A huge-cased clock, painted in the floral Rosemaligen style, hulks in the corner. In another room, I find a piano and ornate, peach-pink upholstered furniture. With a pale light sifting in through the curtains, the place reminds me of the abandoned dacha that became the winter hideout of Omar Sharif and Julie Christie in the film *Doctor Zhivago*, where Zhivago penned his poems about Lara.

Inspired by this image, it occurs to me that Kongsvold would be a good place to get some writing done. The late Bruce Chatwin once wrote an essay called "A Tower in Tuscany," in which he divided writers into two distinct groups: those who stay put and those who move on. Examples of writers who stay put are Tolstoy, Proust, and Zola. In the "Moving-On" category, he put writers like Melville, Hemingway, and Dostoevsky. Chatwin classed himself as a Mover-On, no surprise from a man who wrote on topics as wide-ranging as Patagonia and the Australian Outback.

The restless creativity of the Mover-On is clearly more romantic than the idea of Proust holed up in his cork-walled room and drinking forty cups of coffee per day.

I tried the wandering life for a while. I lived on an island called Lipari, just off the northeast tip of Sicily. I stayed at a pensione called the Villa Diana, run by a Swiss expatriate named Herr Hunsiker. I lived for nineteen dollars a day in a room with no glass on the windows, only shutters, which I kept open at night so that I could smell the lemon trees that grew in the garden outside. All day I wrote facing the wall of my room, pausing only long enough to wander down the hill for lunch, which was always the same, a rice ball with an egg inside called an *arancini* and a cup of frozen lemonade called *granite a limone*. At night, I would stare from the balcony across the Strait of Messina to the lights of the Sicilian mainland, and I would write some more.

I also lived down in Morocco, in a town on the southern coast called Essaouira, which was once the great slave-trading fortress of Mogador. I stayed in a room on the roof of the Hotel Smara, living off bread, apricot jam, and oranges. In the evenings, I would wander down narrow streets that echoed with the sound of the ocean, past blue-shuttered windows through which I smelled mint tea, saffron, and the fiery red paste called *harissa*, wafting on the hashish-foggy air.

It was beautiful, of course, to come adrift from the world that I knew and lose myself among cultures so distant from my own. But there was a heavy price to pay for living the solitary existence of a writer. And it is solitary. A writer writes alone, and if you don't have the work to show for it, you cannot call yourself a writer.

The cost is that a skeletal loneliness appears when you spend more time with people you have invented than with people who are real. You begin to lose track of which world is real, the one whose sun beats down so hard and bright that you are blinded by the white of the page on which you write and must wear glasses as dark as a blind man's in order to see the words that you are forming, or the one you have created like an oasis deep inside yourself.

In the end, I decided to stay put, having reached the conclusion that what you are doing each day is more important than where you are doing it, and that the best thing for a writer is, in the end, to get a good night's sleep.

But here, in Kongsvold, it strikes me that I might find both the romance and the peace of mind. My room looks out on a buttercup garden. Far from home, it is, but still familiar. A fine rain begins to fall. I sit by the open window, breathing the watery air, wondering what it would be like not to go home.

I MUST HAVE FALLEN ASLEEP. It seems as if I just blinked, but two hours have gone by. The dining room is in full swing by the time I get down there.

My waitress is a tall woman with freckles, blue eyes, and hair as dark and shiny as the feathers of a starling. She wears a white T-shirt and a traditional-looking red dress with ornate clips on the front. I fall quietly in love with her during the meal, and through some miscommunication get it in my head that her name is Matilda. Then I notice that the wine she has brought me to drink is also called Matilda. I am too shy to ask her real name. Perhaps they are both called Matilda, but I doubt it.

I eat salmon with cream sauce and dill, while outside in the dusk a harder rain is falling now. The buttercups glow like fireflies in the half light.

After the meal, I wander in to the sitting room for a brandy. Someone is playing the piano. It is a far cry from the traditional Scandinavian drinking ritual of skoaling, in which glasses are repeatedly filled with Akevitt, preferably the Norwegian brand of Linje Akevitt, a kind of vodka flavored with caraway seeds. Before drinking, it is customary to fix your gaze upon another guest, make fierce eye contact, knock back the drink, and then, lowering the glass to the level of your chest, make eye contact again and nod to show the deed is done. Accompanying this is the traditional song "Helan Gor," which means "Hell and Guts." This might have something to do with the fact that, after a dozen shots of Akevitt, you might feel as if Hell has in fact relocated to your guts.

Ensconced on the couch, the brandy glass warming against my palm, I slowly fall back out of love with Matilda. Other thoughts intrude. Tomorrow is my last day in the mountains. Then I will be heading back to Oslo, where I'll take on the final challenge of this journey. I have mixed feelings about it. Much of what I've grown to love out here revolves around the timelessness of this landscape. With so little to show man's impact on the environment, it has been easy to imagine the human dramas that played out here decades or centuries before. Large gaps remain in my understanding of that past. I cannot hope to fill them all, despite the many cultural offerings in Norway's capital city. At very least, I can try to understand the way this country's history intersects with my own, and so perhaps to better understand myself.

I wake early to what I think at first is condensation on the windows. But it is actually fog, as if the whole of Kongsvold has drifted away into the clouds.

An hour later, pockets filled with already-squashed sandwiches, I am heading out the door. Reindeer skulls, nailed to the storehouse wall, leer at me as I pass by. Their antlers look like the spread wings of huge and fleshless birds. Crossing the main road, I head up through a dripping wood of white birch trees toward the high ground, where I have been told the muskox might be seen today.

It is still raining. When I clear the tree line, a raw wind cuts through my clothes. The trail edges along the base of some rounded hills, keeping the river in sight. I keep a look out for muskoxen, struggling to transplant the pictures I have seen onto the misty slopes that rise into the clouds on either side. But the rain and the mist seem to dissolve the world around me, playing tricks with my eyes.

It is a strangely appropriate way to spend my last day in the mountains. Part of me feels as if I have already left, and what I see before me seems to have no more substance than a mirage.

It is the same feeling I had when I recently quit my post as visiting scholar at the Lawrenceville School, just before leaving for Norway. After teaching a fiction class there for eight years, I suddenly could not do it anymore. I was getting too comfortable. The teaching, which had originally been a sideline to my writing, had begun to take over larger and larger chunks of my time, until the writing had begun to seem like the sideline. As soon as I made this equation, I knew it could not go on this way. Or rather it could, and all too easily, and that was the problem.

It is odd how, when you have announced that you are leaving, it is as if you are already gone, even if your physical departure still lies months away. People begin to erase you from their minds, and you walk the halls with a feeling of growing transparency. You remember with a shudder how quickly people who gave their working lives to the institution are allowed to fade away. The memory of an academic institution is about four years. In that time, as the entire student population rotates out, not to mention a good number of the faculty, you will be consigned to anecdote, to one or two things you said or did. The task is to accept it, even to welcome it, not to rage against the dying of the light.

I feel the closing of that chapter of my life; those years spent in the chalk-dusty classrooms, papers graded, verbal jousting in the faculty lounge, the dreary humming of the Xerox machine. All of it passes into shadow, like the folding of a butterfly's wings.

After another hour of plodding alone across the moor, I find myself in a washed-out riverbed, my boots sticky with mud. I have seen no other living thing, let alone a muskox. The colors of the world around me are also washed away, thinned out like water mixed with milk. As I sit down to eat my sandwiches, I am reminded of a painting by Frederick Remington called "New Year on the Cimarron." It shows two bedraggled cowboys gathered around a campfire in a gray and muddy gully. Their horses look old and tired, much like the men themselves. Much like me, too, at the moment.

I decide to head back to the lodge, consoling myself that, in a couple of hours, I will be in that sitting room at Kongsvold, having lounged under a hot shower, scribbling in my old leather-bound notebook. Maybe I will have a brandy, and maybe I will fall in love with Matilda again.

Trudging up the muddy bank, I set out along the path. I haven't gone far when I see them. Muskoxen. Maybe thirty of them. They are on a hillside only a few minutes' walk away. The top of the hill is covered in mist, and they have come down out of it. They linger on the borderline between the fog and clearer air. I can see their huge heads and the pale, curved outline of their horns. Their fur is murky brown, indistinct, as if it is made up partly of the same mist that is hiding them. They seem to have formed a kind of rough circle, with the smaller animals in the center. In this formation, they are idly grazing, and seem not to have noticed I am there.

Reaching for my binoculars, I realize I left them back at the lodge. The damp air and the distance only add to the dreamlike vision. They do not seem real, more like the ghosts of their ancestors, who roamed here fifty thousand years ago.

Then it dawns on me that I am the trespasser here, a ghost from the future instead of from the past. For me, this is the last, most humbling lesson of the mountains. They show you the brevity of your life, but in doing so, they allow you to live it more completely.

Chapter Twelve

These Stones
Are Whispering

AFTER THE CHAOS OF NEW YORK OR LONDON, THE PACE OF life in Oslo can seem bewilderingly sedate. But walking out of the Sentralstasjon into the bustle of Karl Johansgate, after weeks spent in the hills, can make you feel as if you are in the red-hot center of the universe.

Dazed by the throngs of people and boom-chic music pumping from clothing stores, I wander past Peppe's Pizza, McDonald's and the arsenic-green statue of this country's one-time ruler, Denmark's Christian IV. In a musketeer-type outfit, he points regally at a garbage can, while Olso's pigeon population single him out for particularly heavy bombardment.

Weaving past the pedestrians, by pan-piping, poncho-wearing South American street musicians, jugglers, a fire-eater, and a one-man band, I arrive at the Grand Hotel. It is an austere turn-of-the-century building, overlooking the Eidsvollsplass park, where tree-sheltered cafés remind me of those in a miniature Jardin des Tuileries. A small crowd has gathered around a man on a pedestal, painted gold to look like a statue. The sum total of his act appears to be a short bow whenever someone drops a coin in his hat.

In the pillared, marble-floored foyer of the Grand, the red-coated attendant politely ignores my unkempt appearance and my many-pocketed mountain clothes that seemed so in-place such a short time ago and now seem so completely out-of-place. I am escorted up a gilded, spiraling staircase and down a rabbit-warren of corridors to my room. The bellboy tells me the last seating for lunch will be in half an hour and that the sauna and pool are upstairs.

The room itself is clean and functional. Gone are the simplicities of bare wood floors and sleigh-style beds, replaced by wall-to-wall carpeting, CNN on the TV, and gilded bathroom fixtures.

Knowing that I will sleep away the day if I lie down on the bed, I dump my pack and head upstairs to the sauna, thinking to myself that I have done without one long enough.

For those unacquainted with saunas, you must picture a wood-paneled room, rather like a large walk-in closet, in which there is a three-tiered bench. In the corner is a metal container, the size of a large suitcase, that is filled with rocks. On the wall is an hourglass for marking the rotations by which you alternately boil in the sauna and then freeze yourself in a cold shower.

There is very little in my upbringing to prepare me for sitting mostly naked in a very small, very hot room, and sweating until I feel as if my eyes are about to fall back into my head. Fortunately, I have the place to myself, which should keep my humiliation to a minimum.

I spin the hourglass and set the sand running. Then, with a towel wrapped modestly around my waist, I fold my arms like a cigar store Indian and prepare to tough it out.

Soon the sweat is beading up all over me. The metal box for the stones clicks and sighs, and the wooden walls look scorched like those on a stave church. There is nothing to do but think about sweating, or stare through the tinted glass door at the empty bathroom.

But it is not so bad. I tell myself that I can hack it. The sand runs through and I spin the hourglass again. Then, as I squish the sweat from my eyes, I see a woman in a white lab coat standing in the bathroom. She works at the spa, which I saw on my way in to the bathroom. The woman looks at my neatly folded clothes and then peers into the sauna.

I tighten the towel around my middle.

She opens the door and sticks her head in. "Hallo!" she says cheerfully.

When I smile back, sweat drips from my nose.

"Do you want me to turn it on?" she asks.

"What?"

"The sauna. It is not running. Do you want me to turn it on?"

"But it must be running," I protest as I press my hands together, squeezing out more drops of sweat from between my palms. "It's hot in here!"

"No," she tell me. "It is not hot."

"Well," I manage to smear a look of nonchalance across my face, "perhaps you could turn it on, then, please."

Ten minutes later, I am wishing I had never been born. The faint crackling of the stones has now become a gnashing of flinty teeth. The walls are shimmering with heat haze, or maybe it is the sweat leaking into my eyes, I can't tell which. The pink sand in the hourglass seems to have stopped moving altogether. I can barely stand it. In my reeling brain, it occurs to me that of course my Welsh ancestors would have stood no chance against people who did things like this for fun.

Then the sadist in the lab coat returns, carrying a wooden bucket of water with a wooden ladle jutting out of it. "Now it is hot," she says.

I nod, unable to speak.

"This will make it better," she says, and proceeds to ladle water all over the walls. Cobras of steam rise hissing from the stones. Then she thumps the bucket down and disappears again.

The pain is extraordinary. It is the kind of pain by which you judge all other pain in life. Each breath scalds my lungs. Any moisture not wrung from my body flees. I consider fleeing as well.

Just then six Norwegian men show up, all naked except for flip-flops. They crowd into the room and sit with legs splayed, taking turns splashing water on the rocks. They laugh and make jokes. Whenever their conversation pauses—and by now, in my parboiled head, I have convinced myself that the jokes they make are about me—the room itself seems to speak. The wooden walls creak. The stones are whispering.

Only stubbornness keeps me there. It is a matter of national pride that I remain and resign myself to permanent damage. I decide to wait until the sand has run through the hourglass and then head out. No sooner have I settled on this than one of the Norwegians laughingly spins the hourglass so that it twirls around and starts all over again.

Maybe you get used to the being boiled part. Maybe you even enjoy it. It is only after the equally excruciating cold shower that the whole ordeal begins to make sense. You feel as if you have been outfitted with a new body and are convinced that 90 percent of the world's problems could be solved by taking saunas. You immediately make plans to knock down walls in your home and build a sauna there.

When you have recovered from your euphoria, it does occur to you that there is a word for taking so much pleasure from so much pain, and it's not something you should brag about.

THAT EVENING, I HEAD DOWN to the Akker Brygge waterfront, a perfect place to finish up a day in Oslo. A breeze blowing in off the

Pipervika bay rattles the rigging lines of sailing boats tied up at the Radhusbrygge piers. Behind them, on Bulls Plass, trolley cars announce their coming with the clashing-sword sound of wheels on iron rails. Commuters leave the trolleys and immediately board ferries for the ride to Bygdoy across the Oslofjord, which glows like a field of molten amber. Not all are in a hurry. Some find a chair at one of the outdoor cafés, close their eyes, and let the sunset warm their faces.

My impression of Oslo is that it belongs to a culture that is uncomfortable with the whole idea of cities, and created one more for the sake of practicality than for any love of urban life. In fact, there aren't many cities in Norway. The second largest, Bergen, is less than half the size of Oslo, whose population of 500,000 is spread out over 453 square miles. This works out to a population per square mile of 1,103. Compare this to Manhattan's 65,500 people per square mile, or London's 23,500.

Since its founding by King Harald Hardrada in the year 1048, Oslo's fortunes have seesawed between its Danish and later Swedish masters, achieving independence only in 1905. At this time the city was still called Christiania, a name bestowed upon it by King Christian IV of Denmark in 1624, who not only renamed the city but moved it from the other side of the fjord. The ancient name the city bears today, which means the "Field of God," was finally returned to it in 1925.

I cross the Radhussplassen square, under whose concrete slabs must lie that Field of God. Now skateboarders clatter up and down the steps of a somber redbrick city hall that dominates the square. They pause to watch an Elvis lookalike and soundalike contest taking place at a hastily erected stage. There are only four people competing, three most definitely representing the king in his later years. The fourth, a younger man who seems to be in charge of the event, sports an enormous fifties' duck-back hairdo, which makes his head look too big for his body. The Elvises croon "Love Me Tender" at huge and frowning statues of naked women that line the north side of the square. The women remain unimpressed, their Sphinxlike eyes fixed on the old fortress called the Akershus, which dominates the eastern edge of the bay.

The Akershus is a sobering place, as much in its physical presence as in the grim history of its recent past. It was here that the Germans set up their military command for the city during their occupation of Norway. There is still an officer training college here, and men and women in Norwegian green-and-tan-splotch camouflage walk the cobbled lanes inside.

Also within the fortress walls is the Home Front Museum, the Hjemmefrontmuseet, which catalogs both Nazi oppression and Norwegian resistance during the war years. The entrance is through a little house built up near the top of the ramparts. It overlooks the harbor and the long swish of the Holmenkollen Olympic ski jump in the distance. As I walk inside the house, I wonder how they have managed to pack a museum into such a tiny structure, but soon discover that it leads to a large underground complex built deep inside the walls of the fort. Here, in claustrophobic little cells, prisoners of the Reich were kept and tortured before being sent away to concentration camps or shot in a nearby courtyard. There are many dioramas, filled with painted toy soldiers, cotton wool smoke, and plaster-of-Paris mountains, but it is an old and brittle scrap of paper that captures my attention. During recent reconstruction of the prison complex, a roll of toilet paper was found stuffed up the ventilation pipe of one of these isolation cells. On the toilet paper is a message pricked out with the point of a nail, detailing the tortures undergone by a man named Peter Moen, who did not survive the war. You can see the toilet paper behind a plastic screen. I wonder what was going through Moen's head when he stashed the papers in the ventilation pipe, knowing that the chances of them being found were slim. I wish the text of the message had been printed out.

Also in the tunnels of the museum are examples of devices used by the Norwegian resistance to broadcast Allied news bulletins, print underground newspapers, and manufacture weapons. Some of the inventions are remarkable, particularly those used for hiding messages—in the heels of shoes, in loaves of bread, behind the brass WARNING–DO NOT LEAN OUT OF WINDOW sign on a train that shuttled between Norway and neutral Sweden.

Bearing witness to the extraordinary risks taken by Milorg, the name given to the Norwegian resistance movement, is the fact that more than thirty thousand Norwegians were imprisoned by the Nazis, seventeen thousand of whom died in concentration camps.

Understandably, the emphasis is heavily on the German oppression of Norway during the occupation. Much less is said of the fifty-five thousand Norwegians who, by joining the Norwegian Nazi Party known as the National Assembly, backed the puppet government of Vidkun Quisling. The National Assembly was itself backed by a German occupation force whose numbers reached 430,000. Quisling's name became synonymous with treachery among the Allies, but the anti-Bolshevik message he and the Germans preached was heard by portions of all the occupied countries. Volunteers from France, Belgium, Holland, as well as all the Scandinavian countries, including neutral Sweden, joined the ranks of Germany's Waffen SS. They swung on the wrong end of the great pendulum of history, marching into war as the "knights of the empire that would last a thousand years." Now most of them lie in unmarked graves beneath the Russian steppe. The seven thousand volunteers from Norway served mainly under Legion-Sturmbannfuhrer Quist in the Norge Volunteer Legion, which later formed part of the cadre of the 11th Panzer Grenadier Nordland Division. Having fought their way through Croatia and Russia, they were annihilated in the streets of Berlin in May 1945.

It would be too easy for me to view all this in the oversimplified terms in which my own culture views the conflict. As a child growing up in England and America, I received almost daily reminders of World War Two. They appeared in comic books, on TV, in movies, board games, and the plastic models that we glued together. The Japanese and the Germans were, of course, the bad guys. We, the Allies, were the good guys. The Russians used to be good but now they were bad. The Italians tried to be bad but were no good at it. We were told that they put their uniforms on backward and ran away to confuse us. The bad guys, whomever they happened to be, were portrayed as quasi-human, which made their plastic soldiers easier to kill, or watch being killed or read about being killed. One way or another, they were always killed.

Given what I knew as a child, it made no sense to think in any other terms except bad or good. In later years, as a student of history, I felt as if this underlying black-and-white assessment of human behavior persisted in the lessons I was taught.

For us, the Anglo-Americans, there was no middle ground. We had not been invaded. Our armies had not surrendered. Our government had not been whisked away into exile. We did not have to think about what it might have been like to live as collaborators. Anyone who collaborated was weak and deserved to die along with the rest of the bad guys.

But if you happened to be Norwegian, and happened to be in Norway when the Germans marched in, and if you wanted to eat and go to school and travel around, you had to collaborate. The only other choice was to vanish into the hills or risk being sent to a concentration camp. If you wanted to hold on to some semblance of your former life, your only choice was to do as you were told. Of course, there are different degrees of collaboration, but that is my point. It is not black and white. Nor, perhaps, was it as easy to see who your friends were after the British had retreated in confusion, leaving the Norwegian Army to fend for itself.

There is a famous picture of a German Army soldier lying dead beside his half-track in the rubble of Berlin. Clearly visible on the wheel cowling of the half track is the curve-armed "sun wheel" swastika of the Nordland Division. Quite likely, he was a Norwegian volunteer. I think of the Norwegians on both sides of the conflict who died far from home and whose last thoughts must have been of the choices they'd been forced to make in the madhouse the world had become.

Every now and then, you see something that changes your life. The lens through which you view the world is brought into a different focus, causing you to rethink things you once thought you could always take for granted. In the gloomy tunnels of the Hjemmefrontmuseet, my own focus has begun to shift.

Leaving the museum, I find myself back out on the ramparts. The sun has gone now, as have the crowds along the waterfront. The ruffled waves in the harbor look wintery. The statued bodies of the women, which seemed to have a kind of life when the sun was shining on them, have turned back into blocks of stone.

DINNER ALONE IN A FINE RESTAURANT has no appeal. I could have a reindeer steak at the Gamle Raadhus, or try the seafood at Fjordflower, or salmon with sorrel sauce at Bagatelle, but there is something melancholy about a man sipping his wine and carefully spooning his soup, all the while trying to avoid eye contact with people sitting near him.

The answer to this dilemma is the Koffistova. Located just behind the Grand Hotel, it is an unassuming cafeteria serving Norwegian

comfort food. Tonight, this consists of boiled cabbage, boiled carrots, boiled potatoes, and boiled beef served with lingonberry jam
and dumplings the size of oranges. The Koffistova has been serving
up meals like this for a hundred years and is exactly what you want
when you are hungry and on your own and just want a decent meal
without the frills.

For me the atmosphere is familiar, having grown up sliding cafeteria trays past steaming vats of food, while the master-on-duty barked
in my ear: "Move along, Watkins! The kitchen staff aren't going to
tell you what's in the stew. They don't know. No one knows. God
almighty doesn't have a clue, either."

Finding myself a seat in the corner, I glance around to see who
else has comfort food in mind. They all appear to be Norwegian,
mostly elderly, many alone and chewing slowly as they stare into
space with dignified expressions. Three elderly men sit at a table, eating and reading different sections of a newspaper in silence. Now
and then, on some invisible and wordless cue, they switch sections
and go on reading. In a downstairs area, there are also a smattering
of young families, whose children are content to spin the dumplings
on their plates and eat the lingonberry jam with giant spoons. I crack
open my notebook and start scribbling, pausing now and then to
attack the meal.

Afterward, I pass a young English couple on my way out of the
restaurant. They are peering doubtfully through the window.

"I don't know," says the man, with gritted teeth.

"What's wrong with it, then?" asks the woman.

"It's all old people."

I turn to look at him. "I'm not old," I say, and cross the street before
he can correct me. Once I reach the other side, I glance back and am
satisfied to see the woman swatting the man with her chunky
Baedeker's Scandinavia.

Before heading up to my room, I stop at the bar of the Grand Café, where Ibsen once held court. I sigh with satisfaction as I walk into the high-ceilinged space, with its dark mural of Ibsen and his entourage on the far wall. Over by the bar, a piano player wanders her hands up and down the keyboard. The Grand Café has retained its traditional atmosphere without making me feel unworthy of it at the same time.

Most people know how horribly expensive alcohol is in Scandinavia. A lesser-known fact is that it comes in three different strengths. Class 2, which you can buy in the grocery store, is equivalent to what I have at home. Class 1 I have never even seen and do not care to, but Class 3, the strongest, kind of sneaks up on you. After two of these, I feel as if there is a party in my head and everyone's invited.

Following a lengthy tour of corridors, I at last return to my room, where the party comes to a screeching halt. Facedown in my pillow, my last sensation is of the tingling in my skin, a lingering pleasure after the sauna's punishing heat.

BUT THE PARTY ISN'T OVER YET. At 1 a.m., the lights in my room suddenly switch on. So does the TV, whose volume slides to the top of the dial and announces, as if the heat in the sauna wasn't enough, that there is a fire in the hotel.

In an instant, the fog of Class 3 beer is shocked out of my mind. I go through the worst-case-scenario of checking to see if the doorknob is hot. Finding that it isn't, I head down to the lobby, which is rapidly filling with dazed-looking guests.

We aren't there long before the night manager announces jovially that it was a false alarm. From the cursing of some guests, I gather that there has been more than one this past week.

An Englishwoman, wearing a fur coat made of what appears to be the pelts of a thousand squirrels, complete with a fur turban on her head, announces that this is "Not On!" She seems to have mistaken the fire alarm for the international signal that we should all disguise ourselves as woodchucks. She demands to see various people of importance, then stomps upstairs, trailed by her husband, looking like a flasher in his bare legs and mackintosh and clutching a bottle of Veuve Cliquot to his chest.

THE NEXT MORNING, the last of my head-party guests having more or less departed, I am sitting in the Grand Café, eating my breakfast, when a man walks up to me and asks if I enjoyed my sauna.

"I'm sorry?"

"You don't recognize me, do you?" he asks.

Even as the words are leaving my mouth, a little voice inside is begging me not to say them. But it is too late, and I reply, "Not with your clothes on."

So ends one of the shorter conversations of my life.

I WALK ACROSS THE EIDSVOLLSPLASS to the National Theater, where a statue of Ibsen scowls at a taxi stand. An understanding of Norway would not be complete without a thorough study of the playwright. The same is true for the painter Edvard Munch, or the writer Knut Hamsen. But I have set myself a different task in Oslo.

I am growing fond of the city, what little I've seen of it, but am gloomy that the spell will be broken by what I see on the way to Frognerseteren, which lies on the outskirts of Oslo. I'd just as soon not see the suburbs, which can quickly end the love affair one has with just about any city.

Take Paris, for instance. The train ride from Orly airport to the city center brings you past the bleakest-looking concrete sprawl you can imagine before depositing you in one of the most beautiful man-made places on Earth. In order for you to be appropriately amazed by the rest of your time in Paris, you first have to forget what you saw on the way in.

The journey out of central Oslo begins as a subway ride, but quickly rises above ground and just as quickly lays to rest the fears I've had of endless ranks of gray apartment blocks. In fact, within a few minutes the city of Oslo seems to have disappeared completely, leaving the train to climb through an uncongested countryside where it seems as if every house has a view of the tinselly waters of the Oslofjord below.

In my mind, I try to form some equation between this and the world I live in at home. But I can't do it. The whole concept of what it means to live in a city, or in the shadow of one, is different here.

Stepping off the train at Frognerseteren, I find myself on a bare and solitary platform on the side of a hill. A path winds through the woods to an observation tower, from which I am told you can see all the way to Sweden on a clear day. But the purpose of my journey takes me in the opposite direction; down a steep embankment that looks more like a ski slope than a walking trail.

It probably is a ski slope, given its proximity to the monstrous Holmenkollen ski jump, which I saw last night from the ramparts of the Akershus fortress. Holmenkollen is also home to the Norwegian Ski Museum, which is what I have come to see.

Stored at the museum are the artifacts of Roald Amundsen's successful race to the South Pole. Also here are the relics of Fridtjof Nansen's crossing of the Greenland ice cap. Both were not only phenomenal accomplishments but also, unlike similar British expeditions, involved no loss of life.

It seems wrong to me that two men so integral to Norway's accomplishments on the world stage, who have streets named after them in downtown Oslo, should have the relics of their journeys consigned to a few display cases in a ski museum. Despite the fact that it is a beautiful museum, and that the Nansen/Amundsen display is well presented, some of its significance is lost by being swept in with the overall homage to skiing.

Maybe I am missing the point. It is my lack of interest in skiing that links me to Captain Scott, whom Amundsen defeated in the race for the South Pole. Among other factors, it was Scott's disregard for skis that not only lost him the race but cost him his life as well.

I first heard about Scott at the age of ten, when I was at boarding school in England. The dormitory rooms were named after British heroes like Churchill, Shackleton, Chichester, Scott. I had vague notions of who these people were, but only vague. One night, as a master roamed the corridors in his crepe-soled desert boots (perfectly designed for sneaking up on boys talking after lights out), I asked him who Scott was. The master had a square chin and a way of jutting it forward so that his lower lips stuck out, making him look like a bulldog. I still remember the way he leaned against the door frame, hands in the pockets of his tweed coat, and the way the other voices in the room were hushed as he told the story of Scott's trek across the Antarctic ice, and his failure to win the race to the Pole.

"But if he failed, sir," I asked, "why is he such a hero?"

"Because he tried," replied the master, straightening his back, "and because he died bravely."

"Who did get to the Pole first, sir?"

"Amundsen," he muttered, jangling the change in his pockets.

"And who was Amundsen?"

"A Norwegian," he replied.

"Did he die?"

"Eventually."

"But did he die in Antarctica like Scott?"

"No."

"Did any of his people die?"

"No!" The master had reached the end of his patience. There were dorms to inspect, pillow fights to be broken up, voices to be hushed.

"Why not?" I asked, knowing I was pressing my luck but unable to help myself.

"Just lucky, I suppose." With that, he flipped off the lights, warned us not to talk or we would be beaten, and left us alone with our thoughts.

In the whispered conversations that always followed "lights out," we all agreed that Scott must have been very brave and wondered why he had been less lucky than this Norwegian Amundsen.

Luck had less to do with it than I realized at the time.

What happened was this—in 1911, Sir Robert Falcon Scott of the Royal Navy launched an expedition to the South Pole, hoping to claim the place for Britain. Scott was equipped with motorized sledges and horses, which were to be used instead of dogs and skis. What Scott did not know was that Roald Amundsen had also launched an expedition for the Pole.

The race was on.

Both teams set out with the equipment they believed would serve them best, as well as knowledge gleaned from previous polar voyages. Names of ships like the *Karluk* and the *Jeanette*, as well as horrors suffered by the likes of Sir John Franklin and Augustus Greely, were well-known to the members of the Scott and Amundsen expeditions, but the two expeditions had learned very different lessons from the mistakes of the past.

Amundsen and four others (Olav Bjaaland, Helmer Hanssen, Sverre Hassel, and Oskar Wisting) set out from the Bay of Whales across the Ross Ice Shelf on October 19, 1911, hauling individual sleds behind them as they skied and bringing with them more than three dozen dogs, whose wide paws were well suited to traveling across the snow. All but one of the dogs was killed and eaten during the course of the journey, providing the men with the fresh meat they needed to stave off scurvy, a disease brought on by a deficiency of vitamin C. Traveling quickly, the five men arrived at the South Pole on December 14, raised the Norwegian flag and headed back. They reached their base camp on January 25, 1912, having covered 1,600 miles in 99 days.

Scott, meanwhile, was discovering something that should have been obvious before the expedition left England, namely that horses are not suited for traveling across snow. Their hooves are too small to adequately displace their body mass. As a result, the animals continually foundered in the drifts and died of exhaustion, or fell through the ice and drowned. The motorized sledges had not been properly tested and proved to be useless. Most damning of all, the expedition had come equipped with skis, but few on board had received the necessary training for their use. So they marched on foot, dragging impossibly heavy loads over uneven terrain, dangerously weary and suffering from frostbite as well as snow blindness and scurvy. "God help us," wrote Scott, "we can't keep pulling, that is certain. Amongst ourselves, we are unendingly cheerful, but what every man feels in his heart I can only guess." Some of the men, including Apsley Cherry-Garrard (who later wrote a memoir of the expedition, titled The Worst Journey in the World) were forced to turn back before reaching the Pole. The rest, five men in all, reached the South Pole on January 18, 1912. There, they found the Norwegian ensign frozen in the Arctic breeze, as well as a month-old note from Amundsen wishing them well. "All the daydreams must go," said Scott.

Bitterly disappointed, Scott and his men began the journey home. What happened in the days that followed was chronicled by Scott in a diary that he kept almost until the hour of his death.

Capt. Lawrence Oates, or Titus as he was known, became so ravaged with frostbite that he had to be hauled on a sled. An old Etonian and former cavalry officer, Oates had more or less bought his way into the expedition by paying a "subscription" fee of one thousand pounds. Oates was a good-natured man, whose task should have been to take care of the ponies. He had received a wound a few years earlier in the Boer War, from which he was still limping, and confided in another member of the expedition that he was unfit to go on to the Pole. But he was ordered to come along anyway, possibly because Scott wanted a representative of the British Army to reach the Pole, along with a Royal Navy man like himself. On the journey back, with one man already dead, Oates realized that he was now only a burden on the others. He left the safety of their tent one morning, saying, according to Scott, "I am just going out and may be some time." Oates was never seen again.

It was a brave but futile gesture. Scott and the others lacked the strength to go on. Scott wrote, "We are weak, writing is difficult, but for my own sake I do not regret this journey, which has shown that Englishmen can endure hardships, help one another and meet death with as great a fortitude as in the past." He ended his diary with the words, "For God sake, look after our people." With the First World War looming on the horizon, these words proved prophetic indeed.

On November 12, 1912, a search party from the British base camp found Scott and his companions frozen solid in their tent, barely thirteen miles from a food cache which might have saved their lives and which they might have reached if they'd been using skis.

Ironically, one of Scott's underused skis has found its way into the Amundsen display. It is heavy and black, with a rub mark where his foot once rested. How it got there, I do not know, unless it was picked up by Amundsen or left behind at Finse, the Norwegian town where Scott experimented with skis before the expedition set off.

From Amundsen's trip, there are ten-foot-long sleds bound together with string, the red tent (red because Amundsen had determined it to be a color that restored and soothed the eyes of men who had been dealing with snow-glare all day), and a taxidermied dog named Obersten, the only one not killed for food.

Although Nansen was not the reason for my trip to the ski museum, I can't help being drawn to the improvised gear and the story of his journey, which is no less remarkable than that of Amundsen's. Nansen, already a veteran of polar exploration, set out on skis with five others from Umivikfjord on the east coast of Greenland on August 15, 1888. On September 26, he reached Ameralukfjord on Greenland's west coast. Much of the first section of this journey was uphill, for which his skis were equipped with steel strapping and also sections of fur on the underside to give them traction. With winter coming on, and the nearest settlement of Godthab ninety kilometers to the south, Nansen and a man named Otto Sverdrup built a boat resembling a Welsh coracle out of tent canvas stretched around a cup-shaped frame of sticks. They converted their ski poles to paddles, reached Godthab, and had the others rescued before the deep freeze settled on the land. After wintering in Godthab, the expedition returned to Norway on May 30, 1889. As with Amundsen's journey, there were no casualties.

The rest of the museum, devoted to the history of skiing, passes in a blur before my eyes. Leaving the museum, I am so distracted that I walk in the wrong direction, and find myself not at the Holmenkollen station from which I had planned to return to Oslo, but at the Frognerseteren restaurant. It is an imposing log house overlooking the Oslofjord, which gleams like polished tin far below. The logs of the restaurant are tarred black and it is dark inside, the front room dominated by a huge fireplace and bare wood tables with Rosemaligen-decorated chairs. The place smells pleasantly of old smoke, which reminds me of the sandalwood mustiness of church incense.

Over a cup of coffee and a giant meringue that falls to dust as I try to eat it, I mull over what I have seen. I am profoundly moved by the heroism of men like Scott and Oates and Lt. Henry Bowers, whose last letter to his parents once he knew he would never get home, was signed, "your ever loving son to the End in this life and in the next when we will meet and where God shall wipe away all tears from our eyes."

Scott was right. Englishmen can endure hardship. They can face death with fortitude. His generation was synonymous with determination, nobility, and sacrifice for something greater than the individual. It was from people like him that I was taught to draw my inspiration and my heroes.

All the same, I feel as if I have been duped, or have duped myself. What haunts me now is not the lesson of Scott's bravery, but the lesson of Amundsen's triumph. He succeeded by studying the traditional skills of the Eskimo and of Lapland's Sami people, whose millennia of experience in the northern polar realm had taught them the means of survival in a frozen world.

Scott failed, at least in part, because he disregarded the lessons of the past.

Those Englishmen should not have perished out there on the ice. The greater nobility would have been in survival, not in suffering. They should have come home, like Amundsen and his men, to grow old, to see the faces of their grandchildren, to see a thousand more blue skies like the one I see today.

Once more the lens has changed its focus, but the greatest change is still to come.

Chapter Thirteen

The Lesson of the Grail

NOTHING COULD HAVE PREPARED ME LESS FOR A VISIT TO the great Viking Ship Museum, the Vikingskipshuset, than the little golf-cart train that I found waiting for me as I stepped off the Oslofjord ferry in Bygdoy. This contraption would be better suited for a ride through Kiddyland Enchanted Kingdom, with giant mushrooms and motorized elves slo-mo chopping wood outside their gingerbread houses. Instead, with Abba's "Mama Mia" ricocheting off the sunroof, a blue-haired grandma and I spend the next few minutes apologizing as we are swung into each other's laps and the train chugs through the streets of Bygdoy before halting outside what at first glance appears to be a church.

It's strange to see something so Christian-looking sheltering objects which stand for what was once a great thorn in the side of northern Christianity. ("Bitter is the wind tonight," prayed the Irish monks. "White ribbons on the sea. I have no fear the Viking hordes will sail the sea on such a night.")

Much of what we know of these "hordes" comes from early Christian chronicles. How reliable a portrait this represents of the ancient Norse people is open to debate. The closest thing to a period history of the Viking age is a collection of stories known as the *Sagas*, which were written by Icelandic Christians hundreds of years after the events had taken place.

The Vikings reserved most of their own writing for engraving stones to mark the boundaries of property, or for commemorating in runes those Vikings who did not return from their travels. But they did leave us one important document. It is called the *Havamal*, which means "words of the high one" and is supposedly a compilation of sayings by Odin himself. There are seventy in all, and they read like a melding of Sun Tzu's *The Art of War* and Lao Tzu's *Tao Te Ching*. They are rules for survival, both social and physical, for people with no time but the straightest talk:

> GOOD MANNERS: A man shouldn't drink too much. Be sensible or say nothing. None will fault your behavior if you go home early.
> HOSPITALITY: Let a stranger sit by the fire and warm his limbs. A man who has walked out of the hills must have food and clean clothes.
> CAUTION: Always bring an ax when you leave home. You can never tell when a fight is going to break out.

Some of the most compelling descriptions of Norsemen emerged from the writings of Arab emissaries. Ibn al-Fadlan, witnessing the cremation of a Viking chief aboard his Drakkar warship, noted in particular detail the ritual killing of a servant girl who volunteered to follow her master into the afterlife. Of Arab burial customs, the

Vikings had only contempt. "You," he was told, "take the people who are most dear to you and whom you honor most and you put them in the ground where worms and insects devour them. We burn him in a moment, so that he enters paradise at once."

The violence that we associate with the Vikings stems from an often distorted compilation of observations by those whose own capacity for viciousness throughout the ages dwarfs the savagery of the Vikings almost into insignificance. The Vikings were hard people, to be sure, but the Dark Ages in which they lived were a hard time. All civilizations, if they expected to survive, did so by force. Since then, popular culture has done little to adjust that image of the Viking as a monster who killed and raided only for the joy of butchery. I, too, have carried this image with me for as long as I can remember, but it begins to unravel as soon as I walk inside the sparsely furnished museum, where the air is cool and slightly damp and arcing white walls echo with the clopping footsteps of visitors.

The first of three Viking ships, named the *Oseberg*, is held aloft by black metal stakes that connect to iron cradles in which the boat is resting. It seems to float, to be in motion, as if it has been transported through space and time from the middle of a voyage across the North Sea.

The wood looks black and shiny, as if the ship were carved not from wood but from coal. The overlapping planks of its hull seem to sag outward, like the belly of a whale. Its reach or draught, which is the amount it goes down into the water, must have been very shallow. Most Viking ships had draughts of no more than four feet. This design enabled the Vikings to travel up shallow rivers that their enemies thought safe from attack. The symmetrical bow and stern meant that the ship did not have to come about. The raiders would simply row back down the river until they reached a point wide enough where they could bring the boat around. The oars themselves were of different lengths so that they all struck the water at the same time. Impressive as it is, with its length of twenty-two meters and thirty oar-port frame, the Oseberg ship is not a deep-sea vessel but was made for inshore travel.

It was made around AD 850 and was found buried on the west side of the Oslofjord in 1904. The ship served as a final resting place for Queen Aase and her worldly possessions, including a slave girl and horses.

Also in the exhibit are some extraordinarily well-preserved artifacts that were recovered from the Oseberg burial. They include a wagon; various household tools for use in the afterlife; even a peacock feather, iridescent scarab-green; and samples of brocaded fabric, whose gold threads still shimmer after a thousand years underground.

To portray the Norsemen as horn-helmeted maniacs is to blur the fact that they were artisans, too, and some of the most skilled sailors of the ancient world. The rise of their culture, and the indelible marks it has left behind, are tied into the Vikings' ability to build ships like the Oseberg, in whose lines I glimpse the same practical beauty I have seen in so many details of modern Scandinavian life.

The cruciform shape of the museum houses two more ships. One is the Tune, of which only fragments remain, barely enough to recognize it as a boat, which was unearthed in 1867. There is none of the life that still exists in the Oseberg ship.

But the third ship, the Gokstad, is the most impressive of all. Uncovered in 1880, not far from where the museum stands today, the Gokstad has all the sturdiness of a seagoing ship. In 1893, a replica of the Gokstad was sailed all the way to Chicago by a man named Magnus Andersen. Another version, named the Saga Siglar, sailed around the world on a two-and-a-half-year odyssey that lays to rest any doubts about the possibility that these craft could have traveled as far across the oceans as their helmsmen wanted them to go.

In addition to the advantages of a shallow reach (the Gokstad ship measures only six foot four inches from the keel to the gunwale, which is the rim that runs around the side of the boat) and symmetrical hull and stern, what made them superior to other ships was that they were built in "clinker" fashion. This means that their planks were overlapped above a keel of solid oak. Most ships were and still are built around a solid frame, with a solid hull that, if made of wood, is seamed together to provide no overlap. It wasn't until the 1893 voyage to Chicago that the world discovered, or rather rediscovered, the edge that the clinker-built hull gave the Vikings. Viking warships were called Drakkar—dragon-ships—presumably because of the look of their ornately carved bows, which give them a Loch Ness monster silhouette. What Magnus Andersen observed was that, since the hull was not built around a solid frame, but held in shape by cross beams, the design allowed the gunwale to twist as much as six inches from its normal position. The thinning of the strakes in certain places also allowed for uniform flexibility. The result was that the Drakkar could literally undulate like a serpent across the water, giving it unmatchable speed, strength, and mobility. Andersen also found the right-side-mounted tiller or steerboard (from which the word "starboard" derives) to be more effective than the rear-positioned tiller of most other ancient and modern boats.

The Drakkar, and the deeper-hulled Knarr trading ships, ranged in size from about thirty feet to, by some accounts, well over sixty. The Long Serpent of King Olaf Tryggvason was said to have thirty-four oar ports on each side, making it more than twice as long as the twenty-two-meter Oseberg ship.

These ships were what allowed the Vikings to become conquerors, from the first appearance of these northern raiders on the Scottish island of Lindisfarne in AD 793 to what is generally agreed to be the end of the Viking age at the Battle of Hastings in 1066, when the English under King Harold, himself of Norwegian descent, were defeated by William of Normandy, who was also the descendant of Vikings.

But the Drakkar and the Knarr also enabled Vikings to be explorers, and not merely for the sake of plunder. Many Vikings left Norway, and left forever, because they had no choice. The reason has to do with the small amount of agricultural land available in the country. Of Norway's 125,182 square miles, more than 70 percent are mountains. Only 3 percent of the country is cultivated today. In ancient times the amount would have been even less. Add to this the short growing season and the fact that a third of Norway lies above the Arctic Circle, and it is easy to see why Norwegians were forced to go abroad. Also, the line of inheritance established for Norse families meant that the entire farm would go to the eldest son, leaving other sons to make their own way in the world, which in those days often meant raiding. Viking, which is also a verb and comes from the word Vik, meaning "bay," was also a seasonal activity, so men could be both farmers and raiders, depending on the season.

All of the Scandinavian countries played their part in the Viking age. The Danes and Norwegians occupied themselves chiefly with westward expansion, not only raiding but settling as well in northern England, Ireland, Scotland, the northern islands of the Faeroes, Iceland (so-called not because it was covered in ice but in order to scare away future immigrants, so the resident population could have all the land for themselves), Greenland (named by Eric the Red, not because it was particularly green but in order to draw in more settlers), and from there to the New World.

The Swedes headed east, rowing down the cataracts of the River Dnieper to the city of Constantinople, called Miklagard or "Big City" by the Vikings. There the fiercest of them formed a mercenary army known as the Varangian Guard. Russia is named for these Vikings, after the Finnish word for Sweden, Ruotsi, which means "rowing way." The first kings of Kiev were said to be of Viking blood. Their bloodlines are still strong in all these places, many of which still bear their Viking names.

They traveled out across the sands of Arabia, and were known in the dusty streets of Baghdad. They ran their boats up on the shores of North Africa, where they called the black Africans Blamanner or blue men. Their ships enabled them to set up trade routes that still exist today, and the ships that brought them home again were laden with coins from almost every mint in the Old World.

But did they travel even farther?

It was well known that Vikings made their way west to Iceland and Greenland, both considered part of the Old World. But not until 1961, when Helge and Anne Ingstad began excavation of a site in Newfoundland, was conclusive proof of Viking habitation found in the New World. The windswept bay where the excavations took place was called L'Anse Aux Meadows, a corruption of the original French name, meaning "bay of the jellyfish." Here, the Ingstads found signs of boathouses and a blacksmith's workshop (the Native Americans lacked iron-making skills) as well as spindle whorls, indicating that women had also been part of the settlement.

Carbon dating of relics at the site placed the settlement around AD 1000, which ties in nicely with information provided in the Vinland Saga which, although written almost two hundred years after the events it describes, nevertheless describes in great detail the journeys of two men, who were probably the first Europeans to set eyes on the New World. The first was Bjarne Herjolfson, who got lost on his way to Greenland and sighted land to the west but did not drop anchor. When he did reach Greenland, he reported what he'd seen, which inspired Leif Ericsson to follow the path Herjolfson had taken. Ericsson sighted three shores, which he named Helluland ("land of slab rock"), Markland ("land of dense forest") and finally Vinland ("land where grapes grow" or possibly "land of good pasture"). Ericsson wintered in Vinland and, on his return to Greenland, inspired others to make the journey, including his brother Thorwald, who was killed by an Indian arrow. Contact with the Indians, or Skraeling ("wretched people" or "screechers") as the Norsemen called them, proved the undoing of any attempts at colonization. The next Norseman to settle in Vinland, Thorfinn Karlsefni, initially met with success when he was able to sell milk and red cloth to the Indians, who were either Dorset Eskimo or possibly Cree. But things went bad, both with the Indians and with jealousies over women in his own camp, so he was forced to return to his own country. By 1020, both archaeologists and the sagas agree, the Norse had abandoned their Vinland settlement for good.

But was that all? Surely, in the years between Leif's adventure and the writing of the saga that described it, other adventures took place whose stories, or the people taking part in them, were lost.

Tantalizing, although inconclusive, is a penny that was found in the 1970s at what is known as the Goddard Site in Penobscot Bay, Maine. It turned out to be a coin minted in Scandinavia in the realm of Olaf Kyrri, around the year 1070. The coin may have found its way down along trade routes from the Eskimos of northern Labrador to the Abenaki and Penobscot tribes of Maine, but it also might have made that journey in the pocket of a Norseman.

There are many other claims of Vikings sites, ranging the full length of the eastern seaboard of the United States. "A single reliable archeological discovery in any one of them," writes Gwyn Jones, author of a definitive history on Vikings, "could change the picture overnight."

In the meantime, there is only speculation and in some cases outright fraud. A map showing the location of Vinland, purchased for a million dollars and donated to Yale's Beinecke Library, turned out to be a hoax, but not before it was hailed as "the most important cartographic discovery of the century."

Possibility and probability are sometimes separated by great distances, but the more we learn about the ships in which these Norsemen made their journeys, the narrower the gap becomes. Impressive as they are, it was not until 1893, when Magnus Andersen sailed his replica of one of these ships across the Atlantic from Bergen to Newfoundland as part of the Chicago World's Fair, that their true potential was realized.

A hundred years later, W. Hodding Carter and a crew of enthusiasts built a replica of *Skuldelev 1*, an excavated Knorr-type trading ship that had been deliberately sunk in the 1300s in order to block pirates from entering the fjord of Roskilde in Denmark. They sailed it from Nuuk, in Greenland, to L'Anse Aux Meadows, much as Leif Ericsson must have done.

Most compelling of all the possible Norse voyages is a story I heard when I was down in Mexico, in a village called Tulum on the coast of the Yucatan peninsula.

In 1519 Cortez arrived in the Yucatan and embarked on his ruthless subjugation of the Maya and later the Aztec people "in the name of God and the King of Castille." When he asked the first Maya Indians he encountered where he was, they were too busy asking questions of their own and what Cortez took to be their reply, "Yucatan," in fact means "Who are you?" in Mayan.

The Maya soon made up their minds about Cortez's real identity. He was, they informed both him and the rest of the Mayan population, a god named Kukulkan, also known as Quetzacoatl.

It would seem a natural enough mistake to confuse this stranger with a god, especially given the size of his ship, the steel swords carried by his men, and the gunpowder that fired their cannons. The conquistadors made for an impressive sight to the technologically less advanced Maya. But this is only part of the story. The Maya were a bloodthirsty bunch themselves. Their propensity for sacrificing enemies taken in wars, which were more or less a constant state of affairs, their razor-sharp obsidian-tipped spears and arrows, and the sheer number of warriors at their disposal meant that they could almost certainly have made short work of Cortez and his men. Nor were the Maya ignorant of the dangerous potential of these conquistadors. Two Spanish castaways who had found homes among the Maya were quick to warn their Maya friends of the true intentions of Cortez. And yet, despite the warnings, within twenty years, the Maya and Aztec civilizations lay in ruins. By then they had been stripped of their wealth and power, butchered as much by disease as by the sword, and burned at the stake by the likes of Friar Diego de Landa for their refusal to convert to Christianity, while the conquistadors searched in vain for El Dorado, the City of Gold.

One factor that goes a long way to explaining the unwillingness of the Maya to marshall their strength against Cortez, even when they knew his intentions, is the fact that they believed him to be Kukulkan.

But why? There are dozens, if not hundreds of gods in the Maya/Aztec pantheon. What is it about Kukulkan that led to this case of mistaken identity?

Many myths are associated with Kukulkan, which in some case provide a contradictory picture of this god, but most stories agree that Kukulkan arrived among the Maya from the direction of the rising sun some five hundred years before Cortez's arrival. Kukulkan was tall, with blue eyes, fair skin, and fair hair. He stayed among them for some time, but fell afoul of the Nacom when he refused to allow human sacrifices to be made in his honor. Eventually, he left again, apparently promising to return.

As I read about Cortez and Kukulkan, it seemed impossible that this myth could simply have arisen out of thin air. Something had happened to bring it into the collective memory of the Maya. Some one had been there before Cortez, five hundred years before: a tall man with blond hair, pale skin, blue eyes. Around the year 1000, roughly five hundred years before Cortez reached the New World, there was only one civilization that fit this description that could have made contact with the Maya. Those people were the Norsemen.

Immediately the thought had occurred to me, I tried to brush it out of my head. It's crazy, I told myself. The Vikings could never have come this far. But the more research I did on the topic, the more possible it seemed.

It's one thing for the Vikings to have island-hopped from Norway to the Faeroes to Iceland to Greenland and from there perhaps to Vinland itself. But could a ship like those sailed by the Vikings travel as far as the Caribbean?

Not only could it be done, it has been done, and by craft substantially less seaworthy than a Drakkar warship or a deep-hulled Knorr trader. In the summer of 1896, two Norwegian Americans, Frank Samuelson and George Harbo, rowed an eighteen-foot skiff 3,250 miles from New Jersey to Le Havre. Returning to the United States, the steamer on which they were traveling ran out of fuel 250 miles short of New York. The two men lowered their skiff and rowed the distance to the American mainland to fetch help.

Heading in the opposite direction, in January 1969, an Englishman named John Fairfax rowed a twenty-five-foot open boat from the Canary Islands to the coast of Florida, which he reach in July of that year.

Then there is Norwegian Thor Heyerdahl, who in 1970 sailed a boat made of papyrus, christened Ra II, from the coast of Morocco to Barbados. Heyerdahl is most famous for his journey in the Kon Tiki, a raft that he sailed from the coast of South America to the Pacific island of Raroia, not far from Tahiti, a journey of 4,300 miles.

The Kon Tiki itself is housed in a building just down the road from the Viking ships, along with the Fram, the 128-foot ship in which Nansen attempted to reach the North Pole in 1893. The Fram drifted for two years in the polar ice pack, while Nansen and a companion, Hjalmar Johansen, struck out for the Pole. Although they did not attain their objective, they did reach a longitude of 86°/14′N, the farthest north reached at that time.

Most amazing of all is the story of Steven Callahan, whose boat sank roughly eight hundred miles southwest of the Canary Islands, on February 4, 1982. He was cast adrift in a six-foot rubber life raft, with three pounds of food and eight pounds of water. At the mercy of the prevailing sea currents, he drifted for 76 days across 1,800 miles of ocean, before being picked up off the coast of Guadeloupe.

There is no doubt about how far the Vikings could have gone. The question is how far they actually did.

I am sure that somewhere out there, buried in the earth, perhaps nothing more than a silhouette of rust and bone, is evidence that the Vikings ranged much farther than we now can prove.

My mind keeps returning to those ships and how they are virtually all that is left of the great sea power that was the Vikings. There are many other artifacts, of course—swords and coins and spearheads and even whole sections of the Viking age settlement at York—but of the ships that made it all possible, there isn't much more than this. I think about what will remain of our own civilization, what rubble of cities that seem eternal to us now.

In searching for reasons why the Viking age came to a close, it does as well to ask why any great civilization falls. The Vikings foretold their own end in the apocalypse of Raggnarokk, when the world would be consumed in ice and fire, to be followed by a new golden age. In a way, the Viking age did end as they had predicted. In the year 1000, the last of the Pagan Vikings, having sought religious freedom in Iceland, land of volcanic fires and glacial ice, were ordered by Thorgeir the Lawspeaker to be baptized, in order that one law could rule the land.

Whether the Pagan Vikings believed in an afterlife is debatable. It is possible that concepts of hell and heaven, particularly the warrior-heaven of Valhalla, were later add-ons due to Christian influence.

I can't help forging some link between their own lack of self-written history and their belief in a world that would destroy itself. If you add these two together, they point not toward a preoccupation with the future or the past, but with the present. The inability to live in the present is the great malady of modern times, a thing we once knew but have forgotten. Our yearning to recapture it is what causes us, as Thoreau put it, to "live lives of quiet desperation," searching for something that we do not even know is missing.

The discovery of this missing treasure is what binds my journey to the experiences of those travelers who went before me, as well as ancient Norway to the Norway of today.

The neat compartmentalization of history runs together. The past, present, and future all become the same thing. In that absence of time, mortality and immortality lose their meaning. Instead, a new meaning emerges. It cannot be framed out in words. It can only be felt, but its presence and its strength are undeniable.

With a final twist, the lens through which I have been squinting comes at last into a perfect focus. Walking out of the museum, I know that my journey is over.

Twenty-four hours later, I am looking through the porthole window of an SAS jet, thirty-five thousand feet above the Greenland ice shelf.

The day after that, I am back in my study. Carefully I pin my notes to the corkboards on the wall. Then I wipe the dust from my computer screen, turn on the power, and start writing.

Epilogue

I REMAIN DEEPLY CHANGED BY MY TIME IN NORWAY.

It was a journey from which I do not think I will ever completely return. A part of me will always be out there, in the company of Williams, Tjernagel, and the Colony men, whose souls must roam there if they roam at all.

I did not find what I was looking for when I set out. I had held before me, like some image of the Grail, the hope that what happened to me on the fishing boat might be soothed away by going to the land that Arneson had brought to life for me when we were out there on the water. But some nights I still wake up in a sweat, with a taste of blood in my mouth and the feeling of my teeth smashed, only to realize that it was just another dream.

Almost as soon as it had begun, the trip became about other things. But these other things taught me the true lesson of the Grail, which is that the mission always changes and the journey itself is the prize.

Bibliography

Abbie L. Bosworth, "Life In A Norway Valley," NATIONAL GEO-GRAPHIC magazine, May 1935.

Axel H. Oxholm, "Country Life In Norway," NATIONAL GEO-GRAPHIC magazine, April 1939.

Olaf Riste & Berit Nokleby, The Resistance Movement in Norway, Tanum Forlag, Oslo, 1970.

P. C. Asbjornsen and Jorgen Moe, Norwegian Folk Tales, Pantheon, New York. Originally published by Dreyers Forlag, Oslo, 1960.

Mai Sewell Furst and Finn R. Kerr, Norway Today, Dreyers For-lag, Oslo, 1956.

James Graham-Campbell ed., Cultural Atlas of the Viking World, Andromeda Books, Oxford, 1949.

S. G. Bayne, Quicksteps through Scandinavia, Harper & Brothers, New York, 1908.

Bent Vanberg, Of Norwegian Ways, Dillon Press, Minneapolis, 1970.

Russel Kaye and W. Hodding Carter, An Illustrated Viking Voyage, Simon & Schuster, New York, 2000.

Thor Heyerdahl, Kon Tiki, Rand McNally, Chicago, 1950.

Howard La Fay, Vikings, National Geographic Society, 1972.

Ralph Andrist, Heroes of Polar Exploration, American Heritage Publishing Co., New York, 1962.

Bruce Chatwin, What Am I Doing Here, Penguin Books, New York, 1989.

Bjorn Jonasson, The Sayings of the Vikings, Gudrun Press, Reykjavik, 1992.

Odd Borretzen, How To Understand and Use a Norwegian, Aventura Press, Oslo, 1991.

Ingrid and Edgar D'Aulaire, Norse Gods and Giants, Doubleday, New York, 1967.

Per Thomsen ed., Happy Norway to You, J. W. Eides Bokstrykkeri, Bergen, 1949.

Sigrid Undset, Return to the Future, Knopf, New York, 1942.

Ian Heath and Angus McBride, The Vikings, Osprey Books, Oxford, 1985.

Magnus Magnusson, ed., The Vinland Sagas, Penguin, New York, 1965.

Jean Young, The Viking Gods, Gudrun Press, Reykjavik, 1995.

Gwyn Jones, A History of the Vikings, Oxford University Press, Oxford, 1968.

Gywn Jones, The Norse Atlantic Saga, Oxford University Press, Oxford, 1964.

Michael Rohan and Allan Scott, The Hammer and the Cross, Alder Publishing , Oxford, 1980.

Magnus Magnusson, Vikings!, The Bodley Head Press, London, 1980.

William Fitzhugh ed, Vikings, Smithsonian Institute Press, Washington, 2000.

R. I. Page, Chronicles of the Vikings, University of Toronto Press, 1995.

Andrew Stevenson, Summer Light, Lonely Planet, London, 2002.

Friar Diego de Landa, Yucatan Before and After the Conquest, Dover Publications, New York, 1978.

Sara Wheeler, Cherry, A Life of Apsley Cherry-Garrard, Jonathan Cape, London, 2001.

Steven Callahan, Adrift, Ballantine, New York, 1986.

J. A. Lees and W. J. Clutterbuck, Three in Norway by Two of Them, Andresen & Butenshon, Oslo, 2001.

N. Tjernagel, Walking Trips in Norway, Lutheran Book Concern, Columbus, 1917.

Harold Simpson, Rambles in Norway, Mills & Boon, London, 1912.

W. C. Slingsby, Norway, The Northern Playground, Blackwell, Oxford, 1941.

W. Mattieu Williams, Through Norway with a Knapsack, Edward Stanford, London, 1876.

Erling Welle-Strand, Mountain Hiking in Norway, Nortrabooks, Oslo, 1993.

Connie Roos, Walking in Norway, Cicerone Guide Books, Milnthorpe (UK), 1997.

Carton de Wiart, Happy Odyssey, Jonathan Cape, London, 1950.

Jules Brown and Phil Lee, Norway—The Rough Guide, Rough Guides Ltd., London, 1997.

Simon Ryder ed., Norway, Insight Guides, London, 1999.

John Elting, Battles for Scandinavia, Time-Life Books, Chicago, 1981.

Jochen Hemmleb, Larry Johnson, and Eric Simonson, Ghosts of Everest, Macmillan, London, 1999.

Julie Summers, Fearless on Everest, Weidenfeld & Nicholson, London, 2000.

Peter and Leni Gillman, The Wildest Dream, The Mountaineers Books, Seattle, 2000.

Olav Gjaerevoll and Reidar Jorgensen, Mountain Flowers of Scandinavia, F. Bruns Bokhandels Forlag, Trondheim, 1989.

Maps used were produced by Statens Kartverk, The Norwegian Mapping Authority.

Acknowledgments

The author would like to thank the following for their help in the production of this book: Elizabeth Newhouse, Larry Porges, Amanda Urban, John Paine, and Melissa Farris.

About the Author

PAUL WATKINS is the author of eight novels and a memoir, *Stand Before Your God*. A graduate of Eton and Yale, Watkins is currently writer-in-residence at the Peddie School. He lives in Hightstown, New Jersey.

Colophon

The interior text of this book is set in FF Seria Regular, designed by Martin Majoor in 2000 and released digitally by Fontfont. The title type is Lilith light, designed by David Rakowski. Also featured is a mix of Linotype Zapfino One and Two, designed by Hermann Zapf and released digitally by Linotype.

Printed by R. R. Donnelley and Sons on Boise fifty-pound Wyoming antique white paper.

Dust jacket printed by Miken Companies.
Color separation by Quad Graphics.

Three-piece case of Ecological Fiber navy side panels with Sierra dark navy book cloth as the spine fabric. Stamped in Lustrofoil metallic gold.